Praise for Andy Cunningham and *Get to Aha!*

"Andy Cunningham spent years working with the great Silicon Valley technology giants learning how to market innovation. In her remarkably accessible *Get to Aha!*, she pulls back the curtain to reveal the secrets of success."

—Walter Isaacson, president and CEO of the
Aspen Institute and *New York Times* bestselling
author of *Steve Jobs* and *The Innovators*

"Andy Cunningham puts forth a brand-new way to position companies based on her insightful concept of corporate DNA: internal code that reveals the essence of great marketing strategy."

—Regis McKenna, Silicon Valley's original marketing guru

"In *Get to Aha!*, PR legend Andy Cunningham shares her secret for bringing innovation to market in Silicon Valley. It's all about positioning."

—Steve Blank, Silicon Valley serial entrepreneur,
father of the Lean Startup movement, and bestselling
author of *The Startup Owner's Manual*

"It's noisy out there. Andy Cunningham perfectly pulls a Watson and Crick for marketing and helps identify your corporate DNA. If you position it, they will come."

—Andy Kessler, technology columnist at
the *Wall Street Journal* and author of
Running Money and *Eat People*

"Andy Cunningham has been there and done that for many of the critical turns in the technology industry. Consider *Get to Aha!* the core curriculum in the continuing education of any modern branding executive."

—Stewart Alsop Jr., technology pundit and
partner at Alsop Louie Partners

"In *Get to Aha!*, Andy Cunningham shares her many years of experience in Silicon Valley, launching innovation after innovation beginning with the Macintosh. She captures the essence of marketing—strategic positioning—in the digital age."

—Rich Moran, social scientist and author of
The Thing About Work

"*Get to Aha!* is as smart and grounded as Andy Cunningham herself. For more than three decades, journalists have known that in Cunningham they will find someone rich with common sense and ready with straight answers, someone who knows not to waste people's time. This book is all that and more—a crucial set of insights into what it takes for a corporation to know itself well enough to get results—all while staying true to its deeply embedded DNA."

—Katie Hafner, technology journalist and
coauthor of *Where Wizards Stay Up Late*

get to
aha!

get to

aha!

**Discover Your Positioning DNA
and Dominate Your Competition**

Andy Cunningham

NEW YORK   CHICAGO   SAN FRANCISCO   ATHENS
LONDON   MADRID   MEXICO CITY   MILAN
NEW DELHI   SINGAPORE   SYDNEY   TORONTO

1 2 3 4 5 6 7 8 9   QFR   22 21 20 19 18 17

ISBN   978-1-260-03120-1
MHID   1-260-03120-9

eISBN   978-1-260-03121-8
eMHID   1-260-03121-7

Design by Lee Fukui and Mauna Eichner

To my late parents,
for whom writing was the noblest of pursuits
and publishing a book was the Holy Grail

Contents

Foreword

Andy and I met when we were working for Steve Jobs on the launch of Macintosh. She was leading the charge from Regis McKenna, Inc., Apple's PR firm, and I was a software evangelist spreading the good news to developers. My job was to sell the dream. Andy's was to make it credible.

Lately, Andy has been making entrepreneurs more successful with a dynamite approach called "Positioning DNA." Essentially, she postulates that there are three kinds of companies in the world: Mother, Mechanic, or Missionary. When you figure out which one your company is, you are better able to position your way to success.

I highly recommend that you read this book to understand Andy's framework and prepare your company for worldwide domination. Andy is truly one of the people who caused Apple's success, so she could help you become the next Apple!

—Guy Kawasaki, chief evangelist of Canva,
brand ambassador of Mercedes-Benz,
and, oh yeah, former chief evangelist of Apple

Preface

I came to the Valley in 1983 to work for marketing guru Regis McKenna and help Steve Jobs launch the original Macintosh. Both became mentors who profoundly shaped my view of marketing. When Steve left Apple to form NeXT and acquire Pixar, I continued working with him and founded Cunningham Communication, Inc., a nationally recognized high-tech PR firm with a client list that defined Silicon Valley in its earliest days. I've played a key role in the launch of a number of new categories, including video games, personal computers, desktop publishing, digital imaging, RISC microprocessors, software as a service, and very light jets. As an entrepreneur at the forefront of marketing, branding, positioning, and communicating the "Next Big Thing," I have had the opportunity to work in Silicon Valley, the hotbed of the new economy, for more than three decades. I feel lucky to have worked with some of the technology industry's most visionary leaders, to have been in the right place at the right time, and to have had the chance to develop marketing, branding, and communication strategies for game-changing technologies and companies using the approach outlined in this book, which offers a new point of view about marketing and what makes it work.

Get to Aha! is about positioning. And not just plain old positioning either, but DNA-based positioning, which defines a company as a customer-centric Mother, a product-focused Mechanic, or a concept-oriented Missionary. At its core, marketing is a Holy Grail effort to influence opinion and change behavior so that companies can sell more stuff. The good news is that there is plenty of technology and any number of tools available to marketers today to help them in that quest. But technology and existing tools are not enough. It is knowing exactly who you are as a company—understanding your corporate DNA—that can really help you win. Awareness of this DNA provides critical information for creating alignment within the C-suite and across corporate functions.

Knowing your DNA allows you to establish a rational and authentic position for your company within the market. You then can apply that rational thinking to the emotional expression of your company with a branding effort. Start with DNA-based positioning— which is what this book is primarily about—before you even begin to think about branding and you'll have a foundation in place to influence opinion and change behavior in the market.

The payoff? You'll sell more stuff!

This book will show that there are just three types of companies in the world, each with its own distinctive DNA. Understanding that DNA and using it to your advantage are the key to positioning a company in the market and achieving competitive advantage. It is vital to a successful marketing effort. I have come to understand that the single biggest reason so many brand strategy campaigns never make it to market or fail to make any headway if they do is that agencies skip past the rigor required for positioning—what I call DNA-based positioning—and head straight for branding.

Why wouldn't they? Branding offers agencies a chance to flex their creative muscles and win awards. But branding, no matter how clever or well designed, typically doesn't explore the depth of a company's identity and therefore doesn't lead to competitive advantage. Despite the fact that the terms *positioning* and *branding* often are used interchangeably, I believe they are distinctly different.

My DNA-based methodology treats companies like people and offers an authentic way to express their role and relevance in the market. It offers a new and mobilizing perspective on marketing that will help you stand out and build momentum, especially when you are implementing a turnaround or transformation. In many ways, *Get to Aha!* is a follow-up to Al Ries and Jack Trout's seminal book *Positioning*, which I highly recommend as a prerequisite to this one (I like to think of *Get to Aha!* as *Positioning 2.0*). Published nearly 40 years ago and still going strong, *Positioning* was the first book to address the challenge of reaching media-inundated savvy consumers and outlined a revolutionary approach to creating a "position" for prospective customers.

Success today is as dependent on who a company is as on what it does. And when leaders misinterpret their companies' DNA or intervene to change it unknowingly, trouble usually ensues. The recent spate of crises that have plagued Uber, United, and Pepsi are great examples of misalignment between corporate DNA and management action. Knowing your DNA and working with it—rather than against it—paves the path to success. To that end, I offer a simple and easily actionable framework that uses corporate DNA alignment as its starting point. Knowing what you're made of helps you make something of it.

Using real-world companies as examples, including the six case studies that make up Part II, I posit that a company's competitive advantage isn't revealed in a typical branding exercise, no matter how creative it might be. Competitive advantage must result from marketing that starts with great positioning (the expression of a company's role and relevance in the market). I offer a unique inside-out framework that is based on corporate DNA and that shows companies—both B2B and B2C—how to align their positioning and marketing strategy with their true identity. The result of that alignment? Marketing strategy that sticks.

In essence, determining a company's precise position in the marketing landscape should serve as a bridge between its business strategy and the face it presents to the outside world. To ignore positioning and dive straight into branding is like building a house before you've laid the foundation. Instead, a company must position first to align business strategy with DNA and *then* do the sexy branding work to bring that strategy into view. If a company's positioning in the market is wrong, any branding effort, no matter how creative or clever, is probably doomed to failure.

DNA-based positioning is especially crucial for technology companies, which often face industry-specific hurdles in getting their innovations to market. Discovering a company's DNA to articulate its role and relevance is mandatory for technology companies vying for a slice of ever-expanding but highly competitive markets, particularly when the object is to gain traction, manage a turnaround, or achieve transformation. I have used my framework hundreds of times with technology companies; in fact, over the years I have discovered that technology-oriented minds accept and adopt the corporate DNA framework for positioning far more easily than they do the typical "black box" creative process. For this reason, *Get to Aha!* devotes particular attention to helping technology companies pinpoint their competitive advantage in the market (although the principles and framework apply to *any* industry and across *all* types of companies). With technology increasingly a part of nearly every brand today—from pizza delivery to cloud-based customer relationship management—anyone whose goal is to move his or her company into the vanguard of its field needs to take a look at this new way of positioning.

Starting, of course, with the CEO. No matter the organization or industry, the key factor here—as well as everywhere within my DNA methodology and framework—is alignment. And alignment arguably is a leader's biggest challenge. Ken Olsen, cofounder of Digital Equipment Corporation, which created the minicomputer and was the second largest company in the computer industry in the late 1980s, once described a company as a battleship, a mighty war machine. But when you get down to the waterline, where all the work is done, he said, what it actually looks like is a hundred thousand canoes, all going in different directions, with all the paddlers banging their paddles into one another.

What CEO wants this?

At the same time, alignment is critical across the C-suite. Emphasis on alignment is what makes a management team work and what transforms those hundred thousand canoes into a single engine. When a leadership team is aligned and its agreed-upon message has spread throughout the organization, the company operates like a well-oiled machine; it moves in sync, like a school of fish. Or, to adopt the language of technology, it functions like a laser—beams of formerly weak light aligned in a powerful concentration of energy. Concentrated energy gives you the team behind the original Macintosh.

Whatever the business, top-down alignment is the foundation of successful business strategy. When you can get your rowers to stop banging into one another and begin aligning, you've got some power. And when it comes to marketing, DNA-based positioning is what will give you that concentrated power.

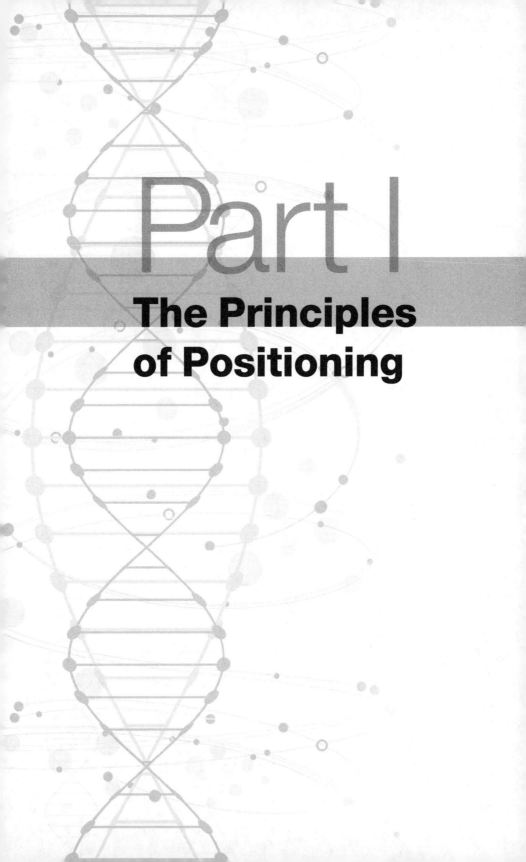

Part I
The Principles of Positioning

Great Marketing Starts
with Great Positioning

Who are you as a company? Why do you matter?

Two simple questions and quite possibly the two most important ones that business leaders face today. The answers, however, are anything but simple. To respond, you must fully understand what—at its core—your company does, what your value proposition is to your most important customers, how you are positioned vis-à-vis your competition, and how to tell your story in a compelling way.

If you find that determining who you are and why you matter is tough, rest assured that you're not alone. Most executives have trouble answering these questions clearly, much less concisely. That is understandable. With so much going on in a company—so many hopes and dreams in development and just as many problems to be solved—it can be difficult to sort the wheat from the chaff. This is exactly why positioning matters: it helps you answer these key questions. Even more, it helps you get to aha!

Let's start with some definitions. Ries and Trout, who invented the concept of positioning in 1969 (and who toyed with the idea of calling their strategic concept "a rock") defined it this way: "Positioning is not what you do to a product. Positioning is what you do to the mind of the prospect. That is, you position (place) the product in the mind of the prospect."

Decades later, this is still a pretty good definition. However, since that time much has been learned about the "marketing method" that results in the perception of a product, brand, or company. Above all, we've come to understand that in the Digital Age, perceptions must reflect substance, not desire or spin. Today's market has too much access to facts and figures to afford companies the luxury of creating customer and prospect perceptions with advertising alone, as they so often did in the 1970s.

Perceptions today are grounded in and sustained by authenticity and thus must start with a new look at positioning. Does the perception of a product, brand, or company reflect its DNA? Is it authentic? This book introduces an approach to positioning that redefines the concept as a *rational* expression of the unique role and relevance of a company, product, or brand in the market: the definitive statement of who you are and why you matter. To ensure authenticity, this statement must be rooted in your corporate DNA. Positioning works in concert with its more emotive sibling—branding—which offers an emotional expression of a unique role and relevance through logos, look and feel, color palette, use of language, tone of voice, customer experience, and design.

Branding, in fact, may well be the most overused word in the marketing lexicon. From its humble beginnings several thousand years ago as a means to identify and denote the ownership of livestock, branding has grown to encompass a complex Madison Avenue activity that covers everything from corporate logos to website design, from customer promise to product experience. Branding today is many things to many people, but for our purposes here, let's confine it to the expression of your company or product with the sole intent of igniting an emotional reaction in your customers or prospects.

To that end, there's nothing like a good tagline to make a company feel like a billion bucks: "Just Do It." "Tomorrow Starts Here." "The Ultimate Driving Machine." Trafficking in a sexy currency of color, design, and voice, taglines touch the inner creative soul and make you feel good about yourself, your product, and your company.

Until you get that tagline home, unwrap it, and try it on. Then you sometimes find that it just doesn't fit. Although it sounded good in the presentation and looked good on the storyboard, in the harsh light of day, it just isn't quite right. Why?

Yin and yang.

The power of this concept from ancient Chinese philosophy lies in the fact that the whole is greater than the sum of the two parts; it is, in fact, the dynamic duality between the two halves that creates the whole. The problem with launching an advertising campaign or developing a website or jumping straight into taglines and other forms of emotional expression (branding) is that branding is only half the story of a company—the emotional half of the story, the emotional yang to positioning's logical, practical yin. Fellow *Star Trek* fans can think Kirk versus Spock. But there can be no yang without yin, no Kirk without Spock, and the same holds true in marketing when it comes to positioning and branding.

So how do you get the yin? You get it via rock-solid positioning that is based on logic (Spock) rather than emotion (Kirk) (Figure 1.1).

The problem is, many marketing and strategy agencies equate positioning with branding. But positioning is not the same as branding. Although the words often are used interchangeably, the concepts are not the same. Positioning is actually upstream from branding; you must determine your ideal position in the market before you work on the brand. Why? Because determining your ideal position in the market results from understanding exactly who you are (your DNA) and why you matter (what you bring to the market that others don't). Your

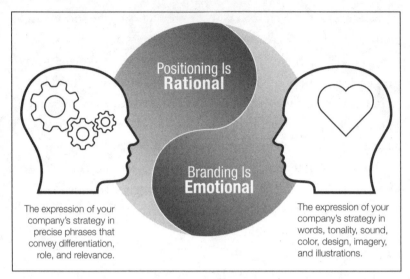

The expression of your company's strategy in precise phrases that convey differentiation, role, and relevance.

The expression of your company's strategy in words, tonality, sound, color, design, imagery, and illustrations.

FIGURE 1.1 Positioning and Branding

ideal position isn't based on a perception you want to create, a brand you hope to build. Quite the opposite, in fact. Brand is derived from positioning; it is the emotional *expression* of positioning. Branding is the yang to positioning's yin, and when both pieces come together, you have a sense of the company's identity as a whole, an understanding of the essence of who and what that company is and what it stands for.

Outline First, Color Second

You know that a brand agency's effort has gone wrong when a company spends thousands, hundreds of thousands, or even millions on a branding project that fails in the market or never gets there in the first place. Instead, the clever taglines and color-coded decks featuring a fancy typeface, cute logos, and elaborate charts gather dust on executive office shelves or eventually are dumped into the digital trash can, never referenced and hardly remembered. After a while, the call goes out to hire yet another brand agency, one that will "get it right this time."

An informal SurveyMonkey panel conducted by Cunningham Collective, my marketing, brand strategy, and communication firm, revealed that among 100 North American CEOs interviewed, *fewer than a third of the respondents felt that the brand strategy work they'd commissioned within the last few years had been at least somewhat effective.* In other words, it failed. The primary reasons for the lack of strategy adoption included an institutional reluctance to embrace change, a lack of understanding of how to implement the strategy, too many competing ideas in the strategy, and the evolution of a business strategy soon after the brand work was completed. One of my clients agreed with this assessment, telling me: "We invested tons of money and tons of hours of our leadership team's time on a branding project with a well-known brand firm. What we got was flashy and pretty, but it's not going to show up anywhere within our company. It's useless to us. It's too fluffy, and our customers won't get it."

I hear this all the time. Companies are awash in branding initiatives that don't work. For some reason, when a company begins the process of "rebranding itself" or "refreshing" its brand, chief marketing officers (CMOs) like to start with the look and feel. Part of the reason for this is that logos and websites are the primary physical currency of a brand, and in today's Internet economy companies are starved for physicality with regard to their brands. The other part is that "eye candy" tends to get noticed by senior leadership teams. It speaks to the emotional side of the brand, something most executives never get to experience; it offers a happy, upbeat distraction from the day-to-day problems that dominate their jobs. Simply put, this kind of branding is fun and refreshing for everyone.

But when you start with branding before digging into positioning—before you understand DNA and the white space in the market that your company is uniquely suited to fill—you are jumping the gun. You are coloring the picture before it has been outlined.

To illustrate, a technology company in the Pacific Northwest reached out to us for help after being unable to differentiate itself in a noisy B2B market. The leadership team hoped we'd be able to develop website messaging that would make a difference. Because we start every engagement with a review of positioning (or of the positioning process if positioning has yet to take place), we put the management team through its paces and came up with a position that was based on the company's DNA. We focused on the primary differentiator of the company's product and made it relevant to the target market.

The team—including the CEO, who had been skeptical of us and our process going into the exercise—was thrilled with the outcome. They saw that with the new position and the means to articulate the company's genuine differentiator they could make a compelling argument for why companies should choose their company over the competition. Woo-hoo! The only problem was that the logo and website had been developed recently by a branding firm, and the work it had done didn't match the company's DNA; in fact, it reflected an identity that didn't really belong to the company. If the branding agency had been hired *after* we did the positioning work, the logo and website would have been congruent with the company's DNA and thus a far better reflection of the corporate brand.

Why did this happen?

Most brand strategy firms start with the branding end of the marketing equation instead of focusing on positioning to illuminate a company's unique identity and competitive edge in the market. They do this because their core competency is design, not business strategy, and when they are hired to "brand" a company, they do the best they can to ascertain its essence and develop a design accordingly. But they don't dig into the DNA of the company, its business strategy, or why it matters in the market. When they think about differentiation, they think about creating design that differentiates and taglines that emote. These are all things that must be done to complete the identity of a company, but they are all things that should be done *after* that identity has been determined.

Push Those Buttons

On the surface, it's easy to see why many agencies skip a rigorous positioning exercise—if it's even on their radar to begin with. Branding is the fun stuff, the place where agencies get to let their creative juices flow. It's the emotional core of marketing and provides an opportunity to deliver the ultimate message, one whose goal is to push as many "feeling" buttons as possible. Branding is the emotional reflection of a company's strategy in words, tonality, color, design, imagery, and illustrations. It encompasses everything from the solid, down-to-earth brown of the UPS logo to the sniffles elicited by Procter & Gamble's "Pick Them Back Up" commercial, which celebrates the first-fall-to-first-medal journey taken by a 2014 Sochi Olympic athlete, one that began with (and paid tribute to) a mother's selfless love for her child. As a result, even if agencies address market positioning, they often equate it with a tagline. And although a tagline is great for delivering the flavor of a brand— "What Happens in Vegas Stays in Vegas"—it's not strategy. It's not positioning. For a tagline to work well, it must be rooted in positioning. In fact, good taglines often emerge from solid positioning sessions almost like magic. But take a peek behind the curtain; that's where you'll find the hard work of DNA analysis and alignment. For example, consider the positioning statement behind that famous Vegas tagline "Las Vegas, once known as a destination for debauchery, is reimagined as a welcoming town where decadent desires can be met." As you can see, the tagline is actually an excellent touchy-feely reflection of this more rational and factual positioning statement—it is an emotional expression of brand.

So although branding is the emotional expression of a company, positioning is the straightforward, rational description of that company's role and relevance in the market, now and into the immediate future. It is also the incredibly important answer to those pesky questions "Who are you?" and "Why do you matter?"

It's All about Sacrifice

Positioning doesn't necessarily expose a company's long-term plans or ambitions, which might well remain hidden until a company is ready to move to the next level of growth. For this reason, positioning is as much about sacrifice as it is about differentiation. Entrepreneurs bringing a product to market probably will never admit it, but what they really want is for that product to be all things to all people: It will solve any problem! It will make you happy! It will change your life! But when it comes to positioning, you have to learn how to sacrifice all the extra stuff, at least for the time being. Instead, what is it that you are going to focus on now? What is it that you're willing to let people see? I use an iceberg analogy to think about positioning. The tip of the iceberg pinpoints your role and relevance in the next year or two and reaches only to spaces that you can own in the near term. That's where you focus your positioning, but it doesn't mean that you give up everything else. It just means that you're not ready to reveal everything to the outside world (Figure 1.2).

Positioning pinpoints your role and relevance for the next one to two years, and reaches only to spaces you can own in the near term.

It may or may not reveal your sales strategy or long-term vision.

FIGURE 1.2 Positioning Is about Sacrifice

Amazon is a great example of this. When Jeff Bezos launched the company in 1994, he had a notion that it was going to be much more than just an online bookseller. In fact, he had a plan for it to be much more than that. In a 1997 letter to shareholders he wrote: "Our goal is to move quickly to solidify and extend our current position while we begin to pursue the online commerce opportunities in other areas. We see substantial opportunity in the large markets we are targeting." He didn't announce his long-term plans to the world at the launch, however, because at that point such lofty goals simply weren't credible. There wasn't enough evidence in the market to support his future vision, and so he started with something he *could* own in the present: online bookselling. Once Bezos had built a reputation for online bookselling, however, he began to add to his vision little by little. Pretty soon Amazon's strategy became clear without his ever having to say anything about it. What formerly had been hidden below the waterline came into full view, but not until the company was ready to show its cards. Today Amazon is the second largest online retailer in the world (behind China's Alibaba, which has a significantly larger customer base) and has completely overhauled our definition of shopping and more. But Bezos didn't start out saying, "We are going to be the online marketplace for anything and everything you can possibly ever want." He started small with something he could easily own and expanded only when he was ready to show the full extent of Amazon's true colors.

Successful positioning also starts with the realization that it is not marketing spin. It's not fluff. In fact, it's the opposite of spin and fluff. Positioning is simple and cerebral. It is a precise explanation of what you offer and to whom, why your product or service matters, and how it differs from the existing alternatives.

Plant Your Flag

Once you've got positioning down, you'll be able to formulate your positioning statement, which highlights the value of your product or service by capturing what you—specifically you and no one else—bring to the market. In essence, a positioning statement is the position your company is taking in the world, the place where you plant your flag. And although planting a flag suggests drama and excitement, a positioning statement should in fact reflect the exact opposite. The ideal positioning statement is factual and logical, maybe even a bit dull. (Remember, the goal is to be 100 percent yin here: logical and precise.) It is an expression of a company's strategy laid out in precise phrases that convey competitive differentiation, that convey who you are and why you matter. It pinpoints a company's role and relevance in the marketplace over the next year or so, highlighting only what the company believes it can own in the near future. It is something only *your* company can lay claim to— something only you can say—and it makes clear you're something to someone rather than trying to be all things to all people.

Take Red Bull, for example. I have no idea what the company's actual positioning statement is, assuming it has one, but I'd hazard a guess that it's something along the lines of "The energy behind great athletic feats." Nothing sexy or exciting there, especially when compared with the company's slogan, "Red Bull Gives You Wings," which is pure yang and broadcasts fun and adventure. "The energy behind great athletic feats," in contrast, is straightforward and yin. It tells you exactly what Red Bull stands for, its reason for being.

Too often, however, agencies overlook the "why" of the positioning statement—the reason for a company's existence. Even if they do provide a positioning statement, it often isn't actually a positioning statement. I recently met with a company that had one of those expensive, never-implemented marketing campaigns stuffed in the back of the chief financial officer's (CFO's) drawer. The agency that had prepared the campaign had offered the following as a positioning statement: "We strive to be agile and flexible and give our customers what they want and need." A laudable goal, certainly, but not a positioning statement. Ditto for another positioning statement brought to my attention during the writing of this book: "Our objective is to deliver customized solutions that equip customers to learn and grow, now and into the future." Yet another laudable goal but again not a positioning statement. Any competitor—and many companies across many industries—could say the same thing. Neither statement describes differentiation; neither addresses role and relevance in the market. What's missing from both? Who you are and why you matter. "We aim to be agile and flexible and give customers what they need" may well represent a company's benefit statement or value proposition, but it isn't a positioning statement. Vague statements often grow out of an attempt to make a company be all things to all people. The result, however, is that you end up being nothing to no one. Done right, a positioning statement lets you know when you've reached aha!

DNA for a Better You

So who are you? And how do you figure that out? People now have tools to understand who they are through DNA, and you can even get your own DNA report from 23andMe, a consumer-friendly DNA testing company based in Silicon Valley (and a former client) that can tell you what your genes say about you: your origins, your coloring, your tastes, your propensity for certain diseases, your ability (or lack thereof) to curl the sides of your tongue. There's even a spot in your DNA, tucked next to a clump of odor-detecting genes, that has something to say about whether you enjoy cilantro or, like 10 to 20 percent of the population, you think it tastes like soap.

Armed with this understanding, you can construct a lifestyle that is aligned with your genes to help you fight off the maladies that afflict your DNA type. Once you know you have a genetic predisposition to heart disease, for example, you know to focus on diet and step up the exercise. A genetic marker for a specific cancer serves as a warning bell for scheduling regular screenings or medical intervention. Know your DNA and be a better you.

Just as people can understand much of who they are from their DNA, so too can companies. Like people, companies are organisms that reflect their creators, their environments, their obstacles, and their strengths. They carry a core instruction set that informs the actions and outcomes of their work. In short, they have DNA. Not chemical, biological DNA, of course, but what I call corporate DNA.

What does that DNA mean for positioning a company to win in the market? Before you can express yourself emotionally, I contend that you must first understand your intellectual and rational side. Just as a person's identity is composed of a rational side and an emotional side, with DNA driving those pieces, a company is compelled by intellectual and emotional elements.

The key to maximizing competitive advantage is to pinpoint that DNA and use it to your advantage, that is, to position your company in the market so that you can win. Your position serves as the bridge between your business strategy and the face you ultimately present to the world. Positioning is an articulation of your overall business strategy as it relates to the customer in a way that reflects your company culture (starting with the CEO). This means that positioning is the key to everything you do once that strategy has been outlined. Positioning lies at the center of every single decision you make, from your go-to-market strategy, to the skill set you seek in your hires, to the way you invest precious resources. It is the foundation for all external messages and campaigns, from branding, to sales strategy, to web copy, to brochure design.

Nearly everyone I've ever worked with using the DNA methodology outlined in this book comes to appreciate the value of starting with positioning. "Our conversation with you and your team wasn't a marketing discussion," said Scott Anderson, CMO of Sitecore, a content management software company. "It was a business discussion." He noted that the easiest, highest-impact action a new chief marketing officer can take is to create a new logo or change the company's graphic design system. "When your goal is to deliver a quick miracle, particularly as a new CMO, that's what you do," he said. "It creates a lot of action and delivers tangible results almost immediately. But tweaking the brand is not the most impactful thing for your company. Positioning is, and that's why it needs to come first."

Only after the management team has a complete and rational understanding of its corporate DNA can it build an emotional narrative that accurately describes who it is and why it matters. (Coca-Cola is carefree. Red Bull is extreme. State Farm is trustworthy.) Only then can it move forward and make well-informed and aligned mergers and acquisitions (M&A), hiring, structuring, compensation, and—most important—marketing decisions. What may seem obvious at first flush is actually a complex process of discovering DNA and working with it to determine a positioning strategy.

A Point on a Map

To begin with, you might find it helpful to think of positioning as a point on a map. In essence, you are selecting a deliberate position within a landscape that is made up of several moving pieces. First there is you and your core DNA in the context of a number of other factors, including the market landscape itself—the area in which you exist, which is your category. In addition to category is community, which includes your customers, complete with all the things they do, say, and believe as well as what they need and want including their influencers; your competitors, including those who currently exist in your category and those who are headed there; and context, which is essentially the trends that shape customers and the competition. We'll cover each of these elements later in the book, but for now, simply put, positioning as strategy asks you to pinpoint your competitive advantage (Figure 1.3).

Positioning is all about building a foundation around that competitive advantage before you take a campaign all the way out to the branding side of things. If the foundation is weak, or worse, not there

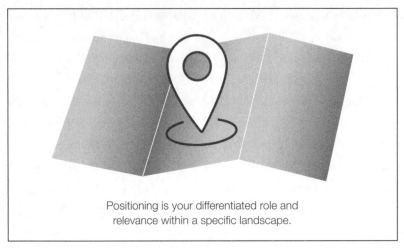

Positioning is your differentiated role and relevance within a specific landscape.

FIGURE 1.3 A Point on a Map

at all, the house will fall. It happens time and again, particularly in the world of high tech. When it comes to marketing innovation in particular, proper positioning is mandatory. If you don't get that right, it'll be difficult for technological ingenuity to take flight. Not because the idea is stupid or the product bad but because it wasn't positioned correctly.

Although positioning is particularly important for high-tech companies, it's the key to the successful positioning of any company. My company learned the hard way not to ignore that cardinal rule when in our early days we agreed to work with a small nonprofit organization. It was not the sort of work we normally took on, but the chairman of the organization was a friend and he really wanted us to create a narrative or story for him (the organization's budget didn't allow for more than that). After a brief discussion, the team tasked with the project agreed to pull together a quick narrative. The cause was good, and they figured that crafting a narrative wouldn't be difficult.

Wrong.

What my team should have told the organization was, "We cannot do a narrative without positioning." There is no getting around the fact that all the components of branding, including narrative, always must be built from positioning. Positioning is the basement foundation, and the rest of the house—the marketing strategy and execution—is constructed on top of it. As a result of time and budget constraints, however, my team jumped straight into branding, which is where the narrative is built. But because the story developed for the nonprofit did not grow out of airtight positioning—it mirrored a competitor's narrative and so ignored differentiation—the project failed. We built a house with no foundation, and, not surprisingly, it fell down. We ended up having to go back and start from scratch, more than doubling our workload. Lesson learned!

Positioning is even important for companies that have no need of advertising or other forms of broad-based messaging. Positioning doesn't just set you up to win, it enables you to keep on winning. You may have only 14 customers, but if those customers make up the entirety of your industry's clientele—if they are the only companies in the world that buy what you sell and they all buy from you—you still need to do positioning. You need to understand what matters to those 14 customers; you need to understand what makes them tick. You need to know them inside and out and anticipate where they're headed next or someone else will come along and do it for you. And of course you must be compelling to them in a way your competitors are not.

Solid positioning is particularly crucial when a company is looking for transformation or a turnaround. A couple of years ago, Avaya Inc. brought me in to help reposition the telecom company, which was working to find its place in a shrinking industry. The first thing my team and I do in a situation like this is learn everything we can about a company by interviewing people both inside and outside the enterprise, from the executive team to the customers—even potential customers who ultimately went elsewhere. At one point during the interview process, I spoke to a customer who pointed to his iPhone and said, "Avaya gives me a complete mobile learning environment." Aha! I thought. That's it! That's what Avaya does. It makes mobile learning environments! And mobile healthcare environments . . . and mobile financial services environments . . . and many other mobile engagement environments. And from that one comment—which later was echoed by a corresponding and heartfelt "Aha!" within the C-suite—we began the process of shifting the company's focus and image. Suddenly it became so much easier to launch and categorize products. We were able to take Avaya's 50-something products and make them that much more understandable not just to the sales force but to every department—and thus to the customer. What had been a jumble of "stuff"—videoconferencing, analytics, audio conferencing, chat, networking, phones, mobile apps, and contact centers—was now neatly packaged under one "mobile engagement" umbrella. We were able to lift the company from the tired category of a unified communications equipment and contact center provider and reposition it as a series of mobile engagement environments. A definite aha!

Aha! Is a Team Sport; Ta-Da! Is a Performance

The power of the DNA methodology lies in its ability to show the true nature of a company and create alignment within the C-suite. The underlying philosophy is that when you understand the essence at the core of the company and work collaboratively with the leadership team to map out the road, magic happens. But here's the important thing to remember: discovering a company's competitive advantage and articulating it simply and elegantly doesn't come from a Don Draper–style magic man going off to a closed room and emerging two weeks later with the perfect tagline. You might get something that sounds cool but upon reflection isn't based on the substance of the company and thus is incomplete.

Taglines offer sexy ways to sum up DNA, but when they stand alone, they offer no differentiation or explanation of role and relevance in the market. "Just Do It" is a great tagline, but it doesn't tell you anything about why Nike is different. It is only when you understand

Nike's positioning and experience it in the market that you understand why "Just Do It" is a powerful tagline—why it is the perfect summation of strategy and positioning. Nike is a lifestyle company that wins by serving a market segment often referred to within the company as the "authentic athlete segment," otherwise known as aspirational athletes. "Just Do It" does a beautiful job of reinforcing the company's strategy and market position over and over because it reflects the company's plan to serve this specific market segment. Everything Nike does every day—the tactics the company deploys to sell more product—reflects the position of owning the authentic athlete.

The articulation of competitive advantage results from C-suite collaboration that is based on logical, DNA-based thinking. In the end you may not even know who had what idea. The breakthrough aha! can—and often does—come from the CFO, chief technology officer (CTO), chief information officer (CIO), or any other member of the management team. This is another reason the entire leadership must participate in the positioning exercise. In point of fact, it can come from anywhere inside or outside the company. Remember, the Avaya aha! came courtesy of a customer I was interviewing as part of learning about the company. No matter the source, however, positioning requires that the C-suite be in complete alignment. That alignment is crucial for coalescing company culture and enabling success in marketing.

Before I developed my positioning framework, I operated as the magic lady, someone who could pull positioning statements and taglines almost from thin air. And here's the thing: clients were thrilled; they loved what I developed. Then they'd leave the room, and that was often that. The excitement would fade away quickly. Why? Because they didn't know where the positioning statement or tagline came from, not really, and so they had trouble executing it. It wasn't enough; what was missing was the meat of the matter. The only way they could understand the message on a deep level was to go through the "boring" process of positioning. Without going through it, no one had a strong stake in the outcome, and so engineering, marketing, sales, and customer service continued as before, each marching to the beat of a different drum, paddling his or her own canoe.

Although a sexy brand package is thrilling to look at, if it doesn't capture a company's role and relevance in the market, if it doesn't capture its DNA, it's little more than a made-up face with no strategy or substance to back it up. This became clear to me one day as I listened to a colleague present the message architecture (message architecture is covered in detail in Chapter 5) of a positioning campaign to the team before taking it to the client. Her slides were highly professional, very sharp and sleek, but something felt off. After she'd gone over her pitch a couple of times, it hit me: the problem with her presentation wasn't that it wasn't good; it was that it was *too* good. The message was getting lost in a blur of lustrous design.

If you present positioning in an overly stylized way, you run the risk of skewing the reaction. Design can make a bad idea look good—or a good idea look bad. Over the years, I've learned that the best way to avoid that outcome is to present the positioning in plain vanilla, as vanilla as it can possibly be, so that a client reacts to the words and not to a whiz-bang design. A lot of agencies will do their research on the market and then come up with something "creative," all gussied up with a great typeface and a fancy logo. They may even set up a dramatic presentation (ta-da!) in which they unveil two or three "big ideas" (a poster-sized ad or Don Draper–style story) intended to represent everything the company is—or at least their vision of what the company should be. It's the company's strategy, personality, look and feel all wrapped up in one shiny and tempting package.

The minute it's presented, everyone in the room oohs and aahs and smiles and nods and says, "Oh, my goodness, that's beautiful, absolutely beautiful." Clients love seeing their brand in such a seductive light, and at first impression it's exciting. It feels like a giant step forward from where they currently stand, particularly if a previous not-quite-right campaign ended up buried in a drawer. High fives all around. Then they go home and tell their families how thrilling the new direction is and sleep well that night knowing they've chosen the "best concept," the one that "feels right."

Once the campaign is in execution mode, however, once it's time to think about publicly presenting the new brand and spending money on it for websites, videos, ads, and PR, companies almost always hit a road bump. A big one. Though it may not always be clear at the moment, too often the fancy and creative concept everyone loved a month earlier cannot stand up as a strategic pillar for the company. It is at best a clever campaign or tagline. But it isn't the thing to unite the company and lead it to truly stand out in the market. Or transform it, which is what many companies look for in their positioning. Why? Because no one on the executive team could see the relationship between the creative execution and the company's strategy, at least not on a deep level.

It all comes down to the fact that if the C-suite doesn't address the basics of positioning first, starting with the DNA exercise outlined in Chapter 3, it won't have a stake in the eventual marketing outcome. Creative taglines and pretty pictures are no substitute for positioning. Branding firms may have ingenious ideas and may even be right about the power and efficacy of those ideas, but if they haven't brought the management suite along on the journey with them, they'll find themselves on a trip to nowhere. DNA-based positioning is the key to ensuring that the executive team maintains a stake in that outcome.

Why go with gut reactions, with what feels right, when you can know with complete, logic-based confidence that your brand is an accurate reflection of your DNA and culture and that it positions you to win in the market? Done properly, positioning creates tremendous alignment among the team members, so much that I sometimes find myself simply helping to connect the dots. Sure, as a company we do a lot of background research for clients, interviewing key stakeholders, both internal and external, to understand foundational elements such as business trajectory, market dynamics, differentiators, customer values, company values, personality, and even company dynamics—all of which feed into positioning. But when the C-suite understands the payoff of the time-tested DNA methodology and has a framework to build on, the hard work of positioning is done by them.

In the end, a company's leadership will buy into a marketing campaign only if it has a hand in its creation. No matter how inspired the campaign, if it didn't originate with DNA-based positioning, bringing the management team along on the journey, it's unlikely to see the light of day in the marketplace. The C-suite has to understand where the campaign comes from. If I just appeared after being holed up in a dark room with my creative team for two or three weeks and said, "Ta-da! Here you go, here's your slogan: 'Just Do It.'" It could be the most brilliant tagline in the world—and I think Nike's 1988 "Just Do It" campaign was indeed brilliant. But if the C-suite doesn't get where it comes from on a cellular—that is, genetic—level, the campaign won't have legs for the long haul. "Just Do It" is marketing genius, but I can guarantee that "Just Do It" didn't come from a creative-only process. It came from the executive team doing the hard work of figuring out who Nike is, what the brand stands for, and what matters to the company. In short, it grew out of positioning.

After positioning is locked up, the process becomes much more of a creative exercise. Once you know you're on the right track, it's time for branding—it's time to capture the company's essence and personality for the world to see in a compelling narrative, complete with all the eye candy that goes with it. That's when you can add all the sexy bits in the form of clever taglines and fun or cutting-edge design. Branding is the dessert you're rewarded with after eating all your vegetables.

The key to winning in the marketplace? Lock in positioning *before* turning your attention to branding. But that positioning process should never rely on a sleek presentation or a magic man performance. Instead, the exercise should create an environment for DNA-based answers to emerge organically within the C-suite. When you know who you are and why you matter, you can articulate a compelling reason for customers and prospects to buy in, and that results in competitive advantage.

2

Core DNA Matters

Human DNA is ineffably complex, composed of molecules called nucleotides—each of which contains a phosphate group, a sugar group, and a nitrogen base. In total, the human genome contains about 3 billion nitrogen bases and about 20,000 genes, but its business equivalent is far simpler, made up of just three kinds of companies. That's it: only three types of companies in the world, each with its own distinctive DNA. Just as I look the way I look because of my DNA and you look the way you do because of yours, companies are what they are because of their DNA, and every organization expresses the DNA of one of these types.

Although it is less complex, each type resembles its human counterpart: Mothers are customer-oriented companies, Mechanics are product-oriented companies, and Missionaries are concept-oriented companies. After having consulted for more than 30 years with hundreds of companies to help them find their optimal position in the market and tell their stories compellingly, I've come to the conclusion that all companies fit into one of these DNA types. I've also learned that knowing which type you are is extremely helpful in developing a go-to-market strategy that sticks (Figure 2.1).

All living species are influenced by a mixture of DNA and environment, and when it comes to corporate DNA, companies are no different. DNA affects a company's culture; its structure; how it measures success; how it hires, trains, and rewards employees; how it allocates resources; how it frames its narrative; and how it decides what brand to send out into the world. DNA is the single biggest factor when it comes to identifying a company's role and relevance in the market and determining its optimal positioning. Your category, community, competition, and the context in which you operate—the environment—also influence company positioning strategies. We'll cover these in Chapter 4.

Mothers

As the name suggests, customer-oriented companies win on the basis of connection in terms of both whom they serve and the expe-

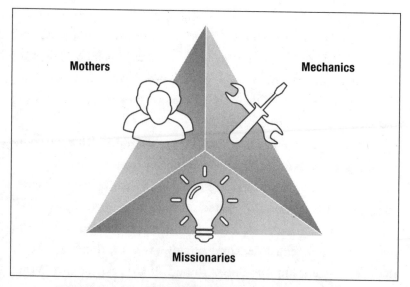

FIGURE 2.1 Core DNA: Mothers, Mechanics, and Missionaries

rience they create. Customer companies measure success by retention, satisfaction, and loyalty, and everything they do—from the way they target a particular market to the way they train and compensate their employees—is motivated by customer needs and those companies' relationships with their customers. I came up with the name Mothers as a result of my experience working with Steve Jobs, beginning with the launch of Macintosh in the early 1980s. (Steve preferred to call the cute little computer by its name; no preceding article—"the" or "a"—allowed.) His vision essentially was "to put a mother in every box" and make the device so appealing and simple to use that Mac buyers would feel that the computer somehow was taking care of them as they unwrapped their purchase, set it up, and entered an enchanting point-and-click realm far removed from the bewildering intricacies of the command-line interface of the DOS-based personal computer (PC). (No Control-Alt-Delete for Macintosh.)

To be clear, Apple's core DNA is *not* that of a customer company, and it never was. The behavior-changing nature of its products puts it in another category altogether. But that's how Steve initially envisioned the Macintosh division, and it's obvious that customer orientation has always been an important component of the company's genetic makeup. Apple is known for its user-friendly products and services, and that's no accident. This is why I use Steve's original thinking to illustrate Mothers. Comfort and ease of use were imperatives early on, from the simple "Happy Mac" smiley face that once greeted users during machine start-up to the self-explanatory trash can icon that lives on in updated form today, both of which helped foster the cultlike following that developed around the company's products. Apple's message was simple and embodied Steve's driving mission: open the box and you'll find a product that is "insanely great"—a catchphrase used around Apple headquarters during the Macintosh days, particularly by Steve, who repeated it probably a hundred times a day—a product that will change the way you work. That is exactly what ultimately defined Apple during the Steve Jobs years. It was a concept-oriented company with the DNA of a Missionary.

Focusing on customer needs is what all Mothers do. For example Hallmark is dedicated to meeting customer needs with cards and gifts for every imaginable occasion, including by embracing what it calls the "new normal" with messages acknowledging stay-at-home dads, same-sex couples, divorced parents, and former in-laws. Or companies such as Zappos, which invests between four and seven weeks in training its customer service representatives and at the end of the training period offers employees a month's salary to quit if they don't feel that the company's customer-first culture is a good fit for them. Nordstrom is another company famous for its service, widely noted for cheerfully accepting all returned merchandise, no questions asked, even items that obviously have been used. Lyft, the on-demand ride-sharing service once known for its now-retired pink grille-stache, is a Mother as well, having worked hard to establish and nurture a customer-friendly reputation to differentiate itself from the infamously cutthroat, scandal-ridden, and PR-insensitive Uber. Although Uber is out to change the world of transportation massively, Lyft's goal is to provide the customer with an experience. In contrast to Uber's take-no-prisoners mantra (Uber's founder, Travis Kalanick, openly admits to having attempted to torpedo Lyft's fund-raising plans), the vibe Lyft seems to be going for is "We're your friend with a car."

No matter the product—which can encompass anything from luxury cars to burgers, from niche magazines to toothpaste—Mothers win by fostering deep relationships with their customers. They then measure their success accordingly.

CHARACTERISTICS OF MOTHERS

Customer companies win because of their relationships with those they serve and the experiences they create. To that end, Mothers do the following:

- Focus on customers in management discussions

- Maintain an outside-in perspective on the world

- Measure success in terms of relationships, not sales alone

Customer Companies

- Initiate tracking studies and market research to get to know their customers

- Create a customer experience that transcends product offerings

- Measure profits against customer segments

- Focus on expanding customer segments and serving needs

- Hire conceptual, personable leaders to close the gap between the C-suite and customers

- Drive marketing through brand and customer loyalty

- Motivate employees to excel at customer service

- Work to ensure that their value proposition delights customers

- Test their value proposition with customers to ensure that it remains highly relevant

Mechanics

Product-oriented companies have a different mission. Mechanics are companies that are determined to build the best products and services and bring them to the masses before anyone else does, with success measured in terms of market dominance. Where Mothers are motivated by their relationships with customers and what they can offer them, Mechanics more often are propelled by technology and what it can do. Read a press release from a tech-based Mechanic, a company such as Microsoft, Oracle, or Intel. With the exception of notifications about executive changes, they tend to address technological advancement: product launches, the newest feature, the latest update. Whereas Mothers pour a great deal of time and money into researching exactly what it is their customers need and want, Mechanics are so confident of the product's superiority that they are convinced customers will want it. They are the experts, after all, and when it comes to the quality of their product or service, they figure they are in the best position to determine what will win in the market.

Although many Mechanics are technology-based, product-oriented companies are found across all industries. Walmart, for example, is a Mechanic, as is McDonald's; their primary focus lies in selling as much as possible to as many as possible, thereby achieving market supremacy. Whether the consumer enjoys the experience, though not insignificant, is often of less concern than it is to a customer-focused company such as Nordstrom. When it comes to a Mechanic (tech-oriented or not), the metrics are all about product performance, market share, category primacy, and benchmark leadership. Whereas a Mother (Marriott, for example) might spend any extra cash on a customer-service training refresher, a Mechanic such as Cisco, BlackBerry, or Walmart would be inclined to allocate that money to product development or sales.

CHARACTERISTICS OF MECHANICS

Product companies exist to build the best products or services and take them to the masses; size matters. To that end, Mechanics do the following:

- Focus on products in management discussions

- Redefine "better" over and over again

- Communicate through winning language

- Project absolute confidence in knowing the product's superiority and desirability **Product or Service Companies**

- Maintain a feisty, aggressive, sometimes egotistical image

- Productize everything and consider it a core competency

- Measure success by market share

- Look at the world in terms of winners and losers

- Promote a sales-centric culture

- Admire in-depth product/technology knowledge

- Organize business units around product lines

- Be almost paranoid about maintaining dominance

Missionaries

Missionaries are concept-oriented; they are the companies dedicated to changing the world and delivering groundbreaking, life-altering innovation, the kind Apple delivered over and over during the Steve Jobs years. Motivated by a creative vision and bold ideas, they measure success by changed behavior and market disruption. Unlike Mechanics, which often focus on new features that deliver incremental change—software updates to address a security weakness, improved solar cell efficiency, a washing machine that uses fuzzy logic—Missionaries are innovation-driven, focused on producing change on a large scale. One great leap as opposed to dozens of small steps. At their core, they exist to change human behavior on a massive scale.

Think FedEx, a newcomer so frustrated by its inability to compete head to head with the air cargo industry that it stepped outside the box and shifted gears, ultimately turning the industry on its head (original Federal Express tagline: "When it absolutely, positively has to be there overnight"). Think Starbucks, the "Third Place" between work and home that disrupted the world of coffee. Think Salesforce—"No Software"—which launched customer relationship management (CRM) into the cloud.

And, of course, think Apple. The sheer number of behavior-changing concepts that have come out of Apple headquarters and its fervently held "failure is fine" philosophy plant it squarely in the Missionary field. As early as 1980, Steve Jobs professed, "It's okay to fall on your face just as long as you pick yourself up pretty fast."

Even one innovative leap would have done it, but under Steve they just kept coming. The Apple II, for example, defined an entire industry. Released in 1977, it was the world's first personal computer. And even though the machine was still at the peak of its success in 1984, Steve reinvented the industry—not to mention how we think about and use computers—with the release of Macintosh, the first mass-market PC featuring a graphical user interface and mouse. (The

Lisa computer, launched just one year before Macintosh, proved to be a colossal market failure at 54 pounds and with a $10,000 price point.) Then, in 2001, a few years after his return to Apple, he launched the iTunes Store and proceeded to redefine the music business.

It's important to note that the iPod, iPhone, and iPad, although hugely successful and impactful, weren't first to market (none was the first MP3, smartphone, or tablet), but they were nonetheless conceptually groundbreaking thanks to their effect on society. Bringing an innovation to market first does not make you a Missionary. What makes you a Missionary is your ability to change the course of human behavior. Not all of Apple's products have changed the way we work and play—the Apple III, the Lisa, even the Apple Watch—but at the end of the day, most of them did. What Steve Jobs did with each of them was to pioneer and initiate monumental behavioral change in people's lives. With the debut of the iPhone in 2007, for example, Steve pushed the stodgy smartphone from its niche within the world of business—a way for companies to keep employees tethered to the office—and launched its user-friendly interface, mobile browser, and app store into the world at large. Our lives have never been the same. Steve was inspiring and fearless, someone who really did "think different." He made the impossible possible and ultimately enchanted the world with his products.

As was noted earlier, during the Macintosh years the mantra throughout Cupertino, Apple's hometown, was "insanely great," and everything about Macintosh was designed to elicit that expression. (Rule number one: incremental improvement was not to be tolerated.) The whole point of "insanely great" was to create a computer that removed the burden of complicated machinery and replaced it with a device that actually enabled the pursuit at hand. But "insanely great" had to encompass so much more than Macintosh and its software. It applied to everything in and around Macintosh: the physical environment, the packaging, the ads, the copywriting. And, of course, the PR, which was my realm.

Like everything else, Macintosh press materials had to go above and beyond "standard"; Apple's determination to be conceptually groundbreaking came through here as well, and quality writing was only the beginning. Here, for example, is how we put together the very first press kit for Macintosh, which was distributed to hundreds of journalists: packaged inside a replica of the iconic white box—designed to hold a start-up disk, a user manual, and power cords—was a series of press releases on the various technological advances in Macintosh; beautiful photos of the computer, the factory, and the Macintosh team; and a Macintosh T-shirt perfectly sized for the recipient. Such a presentation may not seem like a big deal by today's digital standards, but back then, when press releases were written like Associated Press copy and were nothing more than a vehicle to inform the press, it most certainly was. Many of those recipients later reported that the press kit was a joy to receive, and I wasn't a bit surprised. We were missionaries for Macintosh.

CHARACTERISTICS OF MISSIONARIES

Concept companies win on the basis of creative vision and direction and exist solely to change something fundamental about a product, service, or industry. To that end, Missionaries do the following:

- Focus on ideas and customer behavior in management discussions

- Exhibit drive to bring the world a new way of doing things

- Focus on innovation as core to product/service/solution

- Seek to disrupt current market paradigms and business models

Concept Companies

- Foster high-energy environments

- Promote a risk-taking culture

- Maintain a singular vision that everyone embraces

- Engender a passion in people to be part of it

- Employ charismatic senior executives

- Project vision as central to the customer value proposition

- Offer a life choice to employees, who generally share their leader's passion to change the world

- Generate a cultlike reputation

Company Genotypes

Once you know your DNA—we cover how to discover a company's DNA in Chapter 3—it's time to figure out your "genotype," the single biggest indicator in establishing your company's ideal place in the world, the one that will enable you to stand out in your market landscape. Great positioning requires gene expression that is perfectly aligned with your company's core DNA. Just as genotyping is the process of determining an individual's genetic variants on the basis of DNA sequencing, you can "genotype" differences in the genetic makeup of companies. Once again the news is good: finding that specific sweet spot is even more straightforward than determining your DNA. Why? Because once you know your DNA, there are two and only two strategic directions to go—two genotypes for each type of company.

Mother Genotypes: Customer Experience or Customer Segmentation

Mothers differentiate and win because of the experience they offer customers or by focusing on a specific segment of the market.

Customer Experience

Mothers

The first way Mothers win is through Customer Experience, which shows up in the form of customer connections, as seen with Zappos, Nordstrom, and Lyft. Everything those companies do—the people they hire, how they compensate those hires, the way they measure their employees' success, and so on—is geared toward maintaining

Customer Companies

customer relationships; everything they do is geared toward *delighting* the customer.

The Walt Disney Company is a great example of a company that takes customer experience to an unprecedented level. Everything about Disney is designed to make people happy. It offers theme parks, cruises, movies, TV shows, and toys, and each of these outlets works overtime to connect customers to the brand. But what makes Disney stand out is just how deep the customer experience goes. Visit a Disney theme park and you're instantly immersed in a world of scrupulously controlled fantasy where only one Mickey Mouse is ever seen on the grounds, Snow White autographs her name exactly the same way in Orlando and Paris and Tokyo—and still will five years from now—parking lots are named for characters and movies, window displays are at stroller level, disabilities are graciously accommodated, and the logistics of running the park are kept firmly in the background. To that end, loading zones and maintenance areas are camouflaged behind theme dressings, and underground tunnels for the park's actors assure that you'll never see a Pirates of the Caribbean character cutting through Tomorrowland at the end of a shift.

The payoff for Disney? Insanely loyal customers, including many who choose to get married on its cruises and at its theme parks. You might think the parks are predominantly for tourists, but in fact many of Disney's visitors are locals who buy season passes and drop in regularly throughout the year. As D. Bnonn Tennant points out in the marketing blog *Kissmetrics*, diehard Disneyphiles don't just go to Disneyland for the rides, which are fairly run-of-the-mill by theme park standards. Instead, they visit "The Happiest Place on Earth" for the experience it offers, for the shows and the displays and the overall atmosphere; they come to stroll Main Street or just sit on a bench and watch the Disney extravaganza flow by. In short, they come to experience *Disney*.

Facebook is another example of a company deeply committed to customer experience. In this case, however, the beneficiaries of Facebook's bend-over-backward customer service are not its users but its advertisers. Spend any time on the site and it quickly becomes clear that despite occasional polite messages from the Facebook Privacy Team about options to safeguard information, there is a widespread perception among users that the vast majority of complaints about privacy are routinely ignored by the company in favor of maintaining advertisers' access to valuable information. That desire to keep its customers happy determines all of Facebook's business decisions, including which companies it chooses to buy. (Among the myriad reasons Facebook was willing to pay $1 billion for Instagram was the targeted data it could deliver to advertisers.) For Facebook as much as for Disney, the entire enterprise is built around enhancing customers' satisfaction and thus keeping them coming back for more.

Customer Segmentation

The second way Mothers win is by serving a specific segment of the market. Examples include niche publications (*Rolling Stone*, the *Wall Street Journal, Real Simple, Parenting*), luxury automobiles (Ferrari, Maserati, Porsche), and stores and brands catering to individual demographics (Nike, IKEA, Forever 21). Whatever the product, the focus is on appealing to a particular customer with a unique preference or need. For example, Urban Outfitters shoppers demand a distinct style and are happy to reward a venue that caters to their tastes. Similarly, people who favor Tom's of Maine toothpaste (tagline: "Naturally, it works") won't be satisfied with mainstream brands such as Crest and Colgate.

There's a lifestyle element to many Mothers, whether it is an online marketplace for do-it-yourselfers (Etsy) or an energy drink for extreme athletes (Red Bull). Of course, you don't have to be a DIYer to shop Etsy, just as you don't have to be an extreme athlete to drink Red Bull. Either way, the point is to feel catered to as if you were one. Remember the example of Nike as a lifestyle company that wins by serving a specific market segment: the "authentic athlete segment"? Sure, Nike sells serious sports gear to serious athletes, but you don't have to be a serious athlete to wear Nike gear. You can simply *aspire* to be an athlete, and that's every bit as authentic as being a serious athlete. It's all about how you feel in your trail-running shoes. It's about how you feel downing a Red Bull while wearing those Nike trail-running shoes. Customers ask, and Mothers answer, even when it comes to fast food. McDonald's gives you what it gives you—good luck ordering off-menu—but at Burger King you can "Have It Your Way."

Mechanic Genotypes: Product Value or Product Features

Product companies differentiate and win on the basis of either value— what you get for your money—or new and exciting features.

Product Value

Mechanics

Product or Service Companies

When Mechanics are focused on price rather than features, the issue is always one of a value equation, such as "more for less." As was mentioned earlier, this is where you'll find companies such as Walmart ("Save Money. Live Better.") and McDonald's, which eschews Burger King's customer experience model in favor of efficiency in its goal to serve as many customers as possible. McDonald's was so proud of that efficiency, in fact, that for many years it not only kept track of the number of "billions served" but also widely advertised that number. In 2014, however, the company changed its campaign from "Billions Served" to "Billions Heard," an effort to start a dialogue with customers about the food. If McDonald's had been a Mother, this dialogue would have been part of the fabric of the company all along.

Value, however, doesn't have to mean cheap. Value-focused companies also include those selling high-end products and services. Take Surf Air, a small but growing service that offers affordable—relatively speaking—private air travel between half a dozen frequently visited destinations throughout California, as well as Las Vegas. Though a first glance suggests that Surf Air should fall within the Customer Experience genotype, with all the perks normally associated with private air travel, the company is more like an elite version of Southwest. You get the value and convenience of private air travel—meet-and-greet concierge service, comfortable leather seats, convenient parking, no lines, and no TSA or baggage hassle—but you're not going to enjoy the same level of luxury and pampering you'd receive with a high-end Customer Experience genotype such as XOJET. In addition to sharing the plane with other clients, you're limited to fewer destinations and smaller airports, and you fly in propeller planes rather than jets. What Surf Air does offer, however, is a value proposition: many of the benefits of private air travel without the expense. Surf Air is more expensive than commercial, certainly, but it's a whole heck of a lot less expensive than most private jet services.

Product Features

Companies such as Samsung, LG, and KitchenAid are all Features-oriented Mechanics. They're always coming out with new models that do something incrementally better than what you already have on your wall or in your kitchen or in your laundry room: a new and improved immersion blender, for example, or the latest bar-code-reading "smart" refrigerator, which offers four doors instead of the standard two.

Microsoft is another example of a Features Mechanic. Everything it does is geared toward the next new product, the next new feature, the next new update. As a result, when Microsoft considers buying a company, it's typically interested only in other product-oriented companies: Skype, Yammer, Lync. The new companies essentially become new features. You rarely, if ever, hear Microsoft talk about customers. Historically, the message seems to have always been "If you're looking for customer service, go check out our FAQs."

Missionary Genotypes: Next Big Thing or Cult of Personality

Concept-oriented companies also differentiate in one of two ways: they create (or popularize) the Next Big Thing or they're overseen by a Cult of Personality leader who drives revolutionary change seemingly by force of will alone (or, alternatively, a cultlike product that changes human behavior).

Next Big Thing

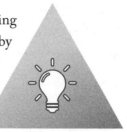

Missionaries that win with the Next Big Thing do it via a creative vision (e.g., Starbucks) or by completely changing the behavior of an industry (FedEx). Their entire reason for existing is to change some fundamental premise about a product, service, or industry. Very often Missionaries are companies in the early stages of life, and some are category creators. This, of course, is where many of Silicon Valley's biggest names show up: Apple, Tesla, Alphabet (formerly Google), Salesforce, and Twitter.

It's also where you'll find Uber, the on-demand car service that launched the Next Big Thing in transportation when it released a revolutionary ride-sharing app in 2010 that required nothing more than the push of a button to call for a car. Like all of its Next Big Thing predecessors, Uber wasn't the first ride-sharing solution. Nonetheless, it was—and still is—out to change behavior and transform the world. (Next up for Uber: UberCHOPPER, an on-demand helicopter service.) And if Uber's founder and former CEO leaves a few bodies in his wake, garnering a rash of negative publicity along the way, well, that's just business. Also, note that changing human behavior by launching something new does not necessarily mean that you were first to market with the change. As we'll discuss in greater detail later in the book, it may be that you were second or third or even fourth to market and, after witnessing failure at some level or another, simply figured out what to do to get it right. Most of the innovations we enjoy today are attributed to the companies that commercialized them, not those that invented them.

Cult of Personality

But there's something more when it comes to Missionaries. What is it that makes a company such as Tesla or Apple so intriguing? What is it about Virgin and Salesforce that makes them stand out as exceptional? Sure, all are known for groundbreaking, pioneering concepts that change lives and have the potential to change the world. But there's something else, something that transcends innovation. Each is also famous for having an outsize, charismatic leader who fomented revolution seemingly by sheer force of will—what I call a Cult of Personality leader.

No matter the degree of magnetism, all Cult of Personality leaders have at least three things in common: a passion for a chosen field (or fields), an outsize vision, and a drive to change behavior. Changing behavior, in fact, frequently leads to the formation of a movement such as the one created by Howard Schultz, the chairman and CEO of Starbucks. In addition to having disrupted the world of coffee by launching Starbucks as the Next Big Thing—the "Third Place" next to work and home—he is a Cult of Personality leader, though one who is less recognizable on the public stage. Over the years Schultz has created a movement around implementing ethical and sustainable coffee-sourcing and environmental practices and advocating for employees and their families. To that end, Starbucks has offered full health benefits to eligible full- and part-time employees, including (as far back as 1988) coverage for domestic partners. In addition, the company was the first privately owned firm to offer a stock option program that included part-time employees. It also launched the Starbucks College Achievement Plan to enable full-tuition coverage for all four years of an undergraduate degree to qualifying Starbucks partners (the company's moniker for employees). Finally, Starbucks committed to hiring thousands of refugees and military veterans and their families in the coming years. In all, Schultz has created a movement that has resulted in people looking at their jobs and careers differently—even looking at their lives differently. And all without putting his personality out there in a larger-than-life way.

In contrast, Steve Jobs was never out to create a movement. Instead, he was all about creating products to improve people's lives—

products that were well designed, beautiful to look at, and easy to use. That was his strategy from the get-go, and it worked. Apple products—and their subsequent updates—became must-have items, starting with Macintosh. People who used the computer, especially in the early days, were the rebels. They were the ones who weren't allowed to have Macintosh in the office (because everyone was using IBMs and Microsoft), and so they snuck them in the back door, usually via the creative department, and used them anyway. Essentially, Steve created a cult around his products. Or, more precisely, a cult coalesced around his "appliances"—a movement was already under way—and those in the know had to have one. Once he realized what was happening, Steve capitalized on the cult, further inspiring others to join. "Think Different," Apple's very famous ad campaign from 1997 says it all by honoring people who are crazy enough to change the world.

Having worked closely with Steve, I can confirm that he burned with a singular passion and drive to change the world. I'd never seen anything like it before, and it's something that never left him. Even his frustration and outright anger when he had to deal with someone who just didn't get it—that was all part of the package, and when you were with him, you didn't even question it. Steve was unrelenting in his demands, but his charisma was such that you were so convinced of his vision you didn't think about whether he was right. When he sat you down to talk about what he was doing, there was no doubt in your mind that he was going to change the world and that you were going along for the ride. All he had to do was look at you and you were sold. It didn't matter what he was selling. He reached out with his eyes and pulled you in.

Richard Branson is another example of a charismatic leader, but he relies on the force of his personality and lifestyle rather than his products. In short, Branson himself has become the cult. By using his services, flying his airlines, signing on to a future flight with his space travel company, or visiting his famously posh Caribbean island, customers are immediately stamped with an imprimatur of cool. In fact, it has become fashionable among the "global citizenry" to brag about an invitation to Necker Island, and it is an even greater honor to cavort with Branson there. All in all, his is a different kind of leadership and Branson is a different kind of leader. Either way, you're hooked.

That's the thing about charismatics—CEOs such as Jobs, Branson, Elon Musk, Marc Benioff, and Walter Beech; politicians such as Bill Clinton, Ross Perot, and Donald Trump; even cult leaders such as Charles Manson and David Koresh. It isn't really an issue of whether they're nice or good or even if they're going to be successful, although many Cult of Personality leaders certainly are: Branson made the name Virgin synonymous with "hip," Musk transformed the automobile and is now attempting to do the same with spacecraft, Benioff has created an empire of devotees by nurturing a movement (and now a global ecosystem) to help his customers increase sales productivity, and Beech commercialized recreational aviation as founder and CEO of the Beech Aircraft Company. In the end, however, it's that a significant number of people believe in them, no matter what. When it came to working with Steve Jobs, no one expected that changing the world with him would be easy. But it didn't matter. We were all in.

Not all Cult of Personality Missionary companies have charismatic leaders at the helm, however. Sometimes the product plays the Cult of Personality role, as in the case of Philz Coffee, an artisan coffee shop chain that has garnered a cult following among coffee connoisseurs in the Bay Area thanks to its many and varied flavors. In addition, founder Phil Jaber and his son, CEO Jacob Jaber, have created a cultural frenzy around the product as a result of its renowned pour-over method and engaging, satisfaction-focused baristas. All that, plus the younger Jaber's stated mission that Philz should "better people's day," might lead you to think the company is a Mother. But it isn't. (For starters, no espresso is served—ever.) Instead, Jaber's overriding drive is to change the behavior of coffee drinkers, one neighborhood at a time.

Another example of product as Cult of Personality is Tiffany, a jewelry company established in 1837 and known for accessorizing women the world over. The company has done such an amazing job of using its DNA to help market its products that its signature "little blue box" has become synonymous with delight.

Of the three types of companies, the Missionary category is the one with the greatest overlap between its two genotypes; this is why you'll find companies such as Apple, Tesla, and Salesforce building the Next Big Thing *and* being led by charismatic leaders (when I speak of Apple here, I'm referring to Steve Jobs). Leaders of successful concept companies are almost always brilliant, but they're not always charismatic. Thus, although many concept companies feature Cult of Personality types at the helm, an outsize personality is not a requirement. What *is* required is passion, vision, and a drive to change the behavior of the human race.

Less Is More

Core DNA and the corresponding genotypes offer an opportunity to narrow positioning choices while at the same time ensuring that a company's position is aligned with its identity. Talk about a twofer! Once you know your genetic makeup and the DNA "set" in which you thrive, there are dozens, hundreds, thousands (even potentially millions) of ways to position your product or service: gluten-free snacks for the toddler set, a temperature-sensitive tea kettle that also brews coffee, adventure tours for extreme skiers, light aircraft for commuters. As it turns out, limiting choice around positioning is more than half the battle when it comes to successful marketing and, in fact, life in general. In theory, an abundance of choices is appealing; in reality, however, it can be incapacitating. Studies have shown that despite a belief, particularly in the United States, that there is no such thing as too much when it comes to choice, an excessive number of options can result in paralysis. In his book *The Paradox of Choice: Why More Is Less*, psychologist Barry Schwartz challenges the idea that more choice equates to more freedom and, as a result, more happiness. Instead, he argues, an overload of options can result in increased anxiety, wasted time, and even depression.

Schwartz's research is supported by that of psychologist Sheena Iyengar, a professor at Columbia University's Graduate School of Business and the author of *The Art of Choosing*, and Mark Lepper, a professor of social psychology at Stanford University. The pair conducted one of the best-known experiments in consumer psychology, the so-called Jam Study, which demonstrated that offering shoppers fewer choices results in increased sales. They found that consumers were 10 times more likely to buy a jam if the number of varieties on display was reduced from 24 to 6. The study showed that 60 percent of the shoppers were attracted to the larger display but only 3 percent opted to buy after sampling on average two jams. However, among those who tasted the jams presented in the smaller array (these shoppers also sampled an average of two jams), 30 percent made a purchase.

Researchers have replicated the Jam Study across a variety of categories, including chocolates, financial services, speed dating, and essay writing. In all cases, the study participants showed greater satisfaction with their choices (or, in the case of the essays, a better finished product) when the number of options to choose from was limited. In addition to requiring more time and effort than people are often prepared to invest, being confronted with too many alternatives—known as choice overload—can result in a psychological burden that opens the door to worry about making a bad decision and potentially to feelings of regret and self-blame. Eliminate the excess, however, and the predominant emotion is relief rather than disappointment or the dreaded FOMO (fear of missing out). I tell my clients that it's like walking into your closet in advance of the big meeting and finding just four shirts to choose from instead of a hundred. (Even better, each of those four shirts matches your eye color.) Suddenly, deciding what to wear is simple. It's so much easier to make a decision when the choices are limited, and that decision is probably a better one as a result of being so *pure*. It isn't polluted with other factors such as "I haven't worn this in a year!" or "I have three black shirts; I should alternate them." or "This shirt was so jammed into the back of my closet that I haven't seen it in months—I should wear it today."

It's the same thing with positioning. Too many factors polluting the choice weaken the result; they make the positioning statement a conglomeration of want-to-haves with very little purity or alignment to strategy. This is what leads to the dreaded "all things to all people" positioning: "My product is the first to do X, Y, and Z for market A and improves the performance of X for market B while at the same time pioneering the Y space for market C." Such positioning results in an embarrassment of abundance and in the end contains so much that it says very little.

With this DNA/genotype process you are first learning about and then expressing the genetics of your brand to the outside world. That doesn't mean that your company's other attributes disappear (remember Apple's customer-friendly interface and service), just that they fade into the background. For example, my eyes are green, but somewhere in my background is the DNA for both brown and blue eyes. It doesn't mean the brown goes away, it doesn't mean the blue goes away; in fact, any of my children could have brown or blue eyes. It just means that green is the color that is expressed. Same thing with my personality. I'm generally seen as easygoing, but that doesn't mean there aren't parts of me that are difficult to deal with. But those characteristics show up only occasionally; they generally do so behind the scenes rather than front and center.

In a similar vein and as was illustrated earlier in this chapter, Disney is clearly a Customer Experience company ("Let the Memories Begin!"), but that doesn't mean it doesn't offer awesome products. It does. Just ask any kid dressed in a Belle costume or clutching a stuffed BB-8 droid or Star Wars light saber. Nonetheless, although winning products are a part of Disney's DNA, Customer Experience is its dominant trait—it is its facing personality, the one that best expresses the identity of the company. The other traits remain in the background in support of the dominant DNA.

The idea of expressing specific genes over (and even at the expense of) others can be a tough sell for C-suiters steeped in the idea that there is value in trying to be all things to all people. I recently met with a CEO—let's call him Charles—of a well-funded and promising Missionary start-up. With an eye toward expanding his product line and attracting more customers, Charles was looking for a new way to talk about his company. Possessing an open mind and a can-do attitude, he was intrigued by the concept of DNA-based positioning, so intrigued, in fact, that soon after our meeting he met with his venture capitalist (VC) and shared my thesis. The VC, however, wasn't buying it. He told Charles that as the CEO of a start-up, he couldn't afford to focus on one DNA type over another. Instead, he had to be able to walk and chew gum at the same time—to, in effect, be all things to all people. But here's the thing: being all things to all people isn't easy. Even more, it is the antithesis of positioning. Great positioning is about sacrifice; specifically it is about the *discipline* of sacrifice. Great venture capital, in contrast, is about picking a passionate founder who can lead, timing product-market fit, and identifying resources (such as positioning) that can help turn ideas into businesses.

Spock Versus Kirk

Limiting choice by discovering your DNA and aligning your marketing with it is an incredibly helpful exercise, especially for logic-based thinkers. It takes the discussion out of the ether and places it firmly in reality. After spending the bulk of my career in Silicon Valley, I've come to understand that when you're dealing with technology companies—and with engineers in particular—you need an approach that's based on logic.

As was mentioned earlier, I'm a huge *Star Trek* fan, and I often reference Spock and Kirk in business. In fact, thinking in terms of Spock and Kirk was how I first developed the outline for the DNA methodology. Some 15 years ago I was faced with a particularly challenging technology client in need of a complete repositioning. The company was made up predominantly of tech guys who were 100 percent engineering-focused, and the acting CEO had just moved over from the private equity domain and didn't yet know all that much about the business. During our first meeting with the leadership team, I outlined the way my firm works with clients: I explained that we'd thoroughly research the company and the market and then come up with a positioning statement that would serve as the foundation for how to market the product. As I saw the dubious expressions on their faces, however, it quickly became clear that my usual "magical" method of pulling fully formed ideas out of my head on the spot or going off into a room a la *Mad Men* and coming out with a media-ready campaign wasn't going to fly no matter how good it might be. Or, to continue my *Star Trek* analogy, I wasn't going to win them over with a marketing strategy based on Kirk-like emotion and gut appeal alone. That private equity guy and his team of Spocks weren't remotely interested in magic; they needed to see behind the curtain.

I realized that if I was going to be able to get through to them (and thus salvage the account), I needed to speak *their* language. First, however, I needed to build the foundation for that language. I spent the weekend parsing everything I knew about positioning and mapping out my system—which I'd never formally defined—in codified form: the idea of a core DNA and two strategic directions, or genotypes. Essentially, I reverse engineered my own process, and when I walked back into the company's offices on Monday, I was able to show the management team a step-by-step framework for how we were going to work collaboratively to position the company, first by establishing the company's DNA type and then by determining an appropriate positioning statement that articulated its unique role and relevance.

The reaction was immediate: "That makes a lot of sense!" And just like that, we were off and running. Instead of me telling them where they needed to go, we would map the road together. My relationship with the client shifted in an instant, moving from polite skepticism to cooperative enthusiasm. That was when I understood that presenting a definable, structured method for developing a marketing strategy was the first step in "getting to aha!"

And not just when it comes to the Spocks of the world. Most people like a framework; in fact, many *need* a framework. Despite a cultural love affair with *Mad Men* that lasted eight years, I've found that more often than not people are suspicious of the notion of a bunch of creative types disappearing into their coffee-fueled lair, only to emerge triumphantly after a week or two and announce, "Ta-da! Here's your from-the-mouth-of-God marketing plan."

What's the Big Deal?

Why does discovering a company's DNA matter so much? Is it really a big deal how a company expresses itself? Isn't it just *marketing*? The product should sell itself, right?

In fact, it really *is* a big deal; DNA is at the root of everything when it comes to competitive advantage. Just think about professional athletes and how their DNA influences their performance. Marketing should be a reflection of the substance of a company, not an image dreamed up by the marketing department. If, for example, a product-oriented company creates a marketing platform that is based on its belief that it is customer-centric, that campaign will never—can never—take hold. Alignment is everything.

My consultancy recently faced that very scenario when we took on a Mechanic that wanted to appeal to the market as a Mother. The brand agency it had worked with previously helped craft attractive customer-friendly language for its brand guidelines and website experience but failed to recognize that the company didn't have customer-centricity in its DNA. It also failed to counsel the company on what it would take to change its DNA from Mechanic to Mother. (As we'll see later in the book, it's not easy.) If the brand agency had worked to understand the company as much as it did the customer, it might have steered the company in a more strategic direction.

In fact, it's that unrelenting focus on delighting the customer that can result in so much positioning pain. There's a belief out there—a philosophy—that all companies must be customer-centric, what I call the Customer-Centric Conundrum. Customer-centricity is a popular trend that causes companies to work outside their DNA; it's a fad that's gotten out of control. It's easy to see how that happened. It sounds so warm and fuzzy to delight the customer, to be customer-centric, to listen to the customer, and so forth. Who wouldn't want to do that?

Nonetheless, if you're all about the product—if you're a Mechanic—equal focus on the customer is antithetical to long-term success. That doesn't mean you ignore customers' needs and wants; it simply means that your primary goal is to nail the product before turning your attention elsewhere. Do what you are good at. Focus on your strengths. Serve the customers but don't be cajoled into catering to them if it isn't in your DNA.

We once worked with a Mechanic headed by a CEO with a very strong personality, someone who valued precision, perfection, and maintaining a stealth approach to the market. He was very serious and focused, an attitude that was reflected throughout the company; he and the brand were one and the same. So when a brand agency recommended a lighthearted and humorous video to launch the company, it fell flat. Why? Because the agency failed to understand the DNA of the company, including that of the CEO.

Another interesting example is a brand agency that desperately wanted to build a consumer campaign for a B2B security software company focused on the Internet of Things. The agency was very excited to present the following campaign: "Secure Your Thing." Cheeky and humorous, yes, but it didn't align with the company's strategy or personality. Needless to say, it was never executed.

It's like me trying to be a ballerina. I can tell myself I'm a ballerina until I'm blue in the face, but that won't make me one. I simply don't have the DNA for it. I do, however, have the ability to be a pretty mean racquetball player. That's something I can work with.

Core DNA matters to humans and companies alike that learn to take advantage of theirs.

3

Genetic Testing

What kind of company are you? What is the dominant trait and identity at the core of your company? In short, what is your company's DNA?

As was noted at the beginning of the book, determining a company's precise position in the marketing landscape serves as a bridge between its business strategy and the face it presents to the outside world. That means it is imperative to get the DNA right, since genetic makeup is the biggest factor in identifying a company's unique role and relevance in the market—and thus its competitive advantage. As we'll see in Chapter 4, several other elements go into determining where to position your company in the marketplace in order to win, elements that should work in tandem with your predominant DNA type. But the framework for choosing that position is always built around a company's genetic core.

Happily, the methodology of discovering a company's DNA is generally a lot of fun. In fact, most people really like the exercise. It's like delving into a Myers-Briggs questionnaire and building a personality profile: ESTJ, perhaps, or INFP. You're opening the door to who people really are, and they love that. They love knowing themselves and love knowing that they have a tribe that can help inform their identity and explain their behavior. They love the sense of belonging in a unique way. Isn't that what marketing is supposed to do? Enable a company to belong in a market? To belong in a differentiated way?

Or at least they love the *idea* of knowing themselves. Here's what I often run into when we begin this process: people almost always say they already know their company's DNA. Sometimes they're right, but more often they're wrong. The first thing they do is latch onto the DNA type they desire, the one they think is cool. This is understandable. Just as I might like to be a ballerina, I'd also like to be tall and thin. But wanting to be tall and thin gets me nowhere. Furthermore, if I were to dress like someone who is tall and thin and engage in tall and thin activities (such as basketball or the high jump), I most likely would end up looking like a fool and failing miserably.

Companies aren't any different when it comes to wanting to be something they're not; they are, after all, run by people. Say my team and I are meeting with a company that is really into technology. After we've explained the different categories to the management team, they're likely to nod knowingly and say, "Oh, that's easy; we're a Missionary." Or maybe, having read all the books about how customer care is the key to success, they're set on the idea of the organization being a Mother. When we dig deeper, however, we may well discover that neither is true and that the company is actually a Mechanic. That's how it's structured, that's how it hires, that's how it compensates its employees, and that's how it measures success. Wanting a company to be something else, believing it to be something else—and jumping through hoops to justify that belief—doesn't change the fact that its DNA clearly identifies it as a Mechanic. As a result, acting like a Mother or a Missionary doesn't ring true. It lacks authenticity.

Even Steve Jobs got it wrong early on when he told me he wanted to "put a mother in every box," by which he meant that upon opening an Apple product, the customer should feel comfortable and well taken care of from the get-go. Although operating as a Customer Experience Mother might have been Steve's original idea, an innate drive to overhaul the status quo, create something revolutionary, and change behavior ensured that Apple would never remain customer-centric. As a result, Steve—aided by his charisma—created something far bigger as a Missionary than he ever would have as a Mother: he turned both the computer industry and the music industry on their heads, and as a result, changed what we expect from a computer and how we listen to music. Thanks to Steve Jobs, Apple offered us the Next Big Thing over and over again. And with those Next Big Things came a Cult of Personality that formed around him and his products.

In truth, very few of the companies we work with are Missionaries, but that doesn't stop people from aspiring in that direction, particularly in the world of high tech, where everyone wants to be the next Apple or Alphabet and change the world. Here's where you need to be careful. There is no "good" or "bad" genetic type. There is only what you are. Just as in life, it's what you do with what you are that makes all the difference. Simply put, knowing your genetic type and aligning your behavior with it makes you a better you.

People will look at the outcome of the DNA test at the end of this chapter and say, "Well, we want to be bold innovators, so we *can't* be a Mechanic." Or we'll hear, "We're clearly a Mother, and that isn't what we want at all! We *need* to be a Missionary if we're going to disrupt the market."

No! No! No!

You absolutely *can* dominate a market as a Mother and you *can* be a bold innovator as a Mechanic, just as you can disrupt markets and create new categories as any one of the three DNA types. The point is that you should position your company in accordance with the reality of your DNA. The decision to create a new category, disrupt an incumbent, or find a new way of doing things is independent of your DNA type. But understanding your DNA type and working with it, rather than against it, will make those Big Hairy Audacious Goals easier to accomplish.

Consider Clayton Christensen's theory of disruptive innovation, a term used in his book *The Innovator's Dilemma*. According to the Clayton Christensen Institute, the theory describes "the phenomenon by which an innovation transforms an existing market or sector by introducing simplicity, convenience, accessibility, and affordability where complication and high cost are the status quo. Initially, a disruptive innovation is formed in a niche market that may appear unattractive or inconsequential to industry incumbents, but eventually the new product or idea completely redefines the industry." Examples of disruption include personal computers (which disrupted mainframe computers and minicomputers), community colleges (which disrupted four-year colleges), discount retailers (which disrupted full-service department stores), retail medical clinics (which disrupted traditional doctors' offices), and cellular phones (which disrupted fixed-line telephony).

The important thing to remember is that disruption—also known as "better, faster, cheaper"—can come from any kind of company. There is no question, however, that Mechanics' strict focus on value can give them an advantage over incumbents. Ben Thompson, who writes the *Stratechery* blog, opens an interesting window onto how companies enter and ultimately win the market by targeting competitors on price: "[A] new market entry is laughably inferior, but it's cheap, and it serves new customers to the market. Then, it gets better, and it starts to steal prospective customers from the incumbents. Then, it gets better, and it gets scale, and it starts to poach those most sensitive to the incumbent's high prices. And, eventually, the new market incumbent is straight up superior, yet cheaper, and the incumbent is dead."

By all means be the next Apple or Alphabet. Just remember that you don't *need* to be a Missionary to dominate or disrupt the market. You can be the next Facebook instead, a Mother that in the dozen years since its launch has created not only enormous momentum in the world of social networking but also huge value for its shareholders. Or you can become the next SurveyMonkey, a Mechanic blazing a trail in the "freemium" software industry. You can innovate, you can be a maverick, and you can be a trailblazer even if you're not a Missionary. But the *way* you go about being an innovator, maverick, or trailblazer will be completely different depending on your DNA.

It's not unusual for people to want to be something they're not. That's why we dye our hair or overhaul our wardrobe or change our profession. My DNA may not make me a blond, but my hairdresser certainly can. And that's fine; stepping outside my personal DNA can be a lot of fun. But not when it comes to corporate DNA. That's not something that's easily changed, and presenting your company's best face to the world gets a whole lot harder—with failure a distinct possibility—when you implement a marketing plan that grows out of DNA that isn't your own.

For example, say I want to create a new airline that will blow the doors off what any other airline has ever accomplished. (For the record, launching an airline is a wildly challenging and expensive endeavor, but at its most basic level it works well as an illustration of DNA possibilities.) If I'm a technology-focused Mechanic, I might throw my efforts into disrupting inventory management by implementing a cutting-edge algorithm that adds machine learning to the seat design and distribution process. For me, the whole issue is framed around what I can do with technology to improve inventory and pricing vastly so that my airline comes out on top. Why? Because my Mechanic DNA says that product has to come first, and in this case I'm going to work on the inventory to ensure that the product addresses supply and demand issues before anything else. And when I'm done, the supply chain will be perfected—we'll have that nailed. If the consumer isn't as comfortable on my planes or if it takes me a little longer to get to market, I'm okay with that, because the most important thing to me is that the product does exactly what I spec it to do and that the price is as low as possible because of that; customer experience can come next. In this case, the advantage to the customer will come in the form of cost savings, not experience. As an example, consider PEOPLExpress. Launched in 1981 (and officially known as People Express Airlines), it offered an inexpensive mode of air travel with the focus on systems rather than customers. Its positioning was based on value—air travel for less. Like many other airlines, PEOPLExpress did not survive the cost structures of the airline business, and it was acquired by Continental Airlines in 1987. But it sure gave the industry one hell of a Mechanic shot!

If my corporate DNA is Mother, I'll flip those priorities. I'll be willing to sacrifice a few things on the product end—improved seat design and inventory control, perhaps—to ensure that my relationship with my customers remains sacrosanct. As a Mother, my goal is still to disrupt, but I'm always going to be disrupting from the point of view of the passenger by overhauling the cabin and the service structure to appeal to personal tastes that the customer is willing to pay for. My primary concern is making sure everything I design is geared toward enhancing the flier's experience at the lowest cost. A good example here is Virgin America. It found a way to make mundane, customer-facing experiences sexy and interesting. Under CEO Fred Reid, who positioned the airline as a Customer Experience Mother, ordering food on a plane became cool, sitting in "Main Cabin Select" was desirable, and walking onto an airplane lit like a lounge was soothing. Suddenly, customers were massively clicking "like" about flying Virgin America.

If I'm a Missionary, however, my outlook will be something else entirely. I'm going to say, "You know what? The supply chains might not like what I do at first, and passengers might find the seats a bit cramped, but that's okay. I don't care, because what I'm going to bring to the market is mind-blowing. I'm out to change flying behavior, and once people see our revolutionary plan for a compost-fueled plane that can travel from San Francisco to Sydney in just six hours, they're going to realize they can't live without it. I just know it!" We haven't seen this airline yet, of course. But the first one to use drones to transport people may just have a shot at revamping the entire airline industry and creating the Next Big Thing.

In each of these three scenarios I'm creating a drastically new airline that will disrupt the market and perhaps even change the way society views air travel. But the way I'm coming at the decision-making process—how and where to focus my efforts and resources—is based entirely on my company's DNA.

The whole idea here is that when you know who you are, you begin to realize that DNA is not simply an approach to marketing: DNA is at the core of it. The genetic makeup of your company means you're predisposed to do things a certain way. If you have to make a three-way decision among changing behavior, protecting the customer, and getting the technology right the first time, which would you favor in every decision? Which of the three do your horizontal and vertical business practices favor? How about your hiring decisions? Your compensation decisions? Your product design and road map decisions? Look closely and you'll usually see a common thread running through everything you do as a company, and it all comes down to your DNA: you're a Mother, you're a Mechanic, or you're a Missionary.

A final point: the fact that you are a Missionary airline doesn't mean you ignore the product or the customer experience. Far from it, as illustrated in Chapter 2 by Charles and the VC who counseled him to ignore DNA-based positioning and instead try to be all things to all people. It simply means that the face you present to the world reflects your Missionary genes and highlights your dominant traits. A high-quality product and an acceptable experience are important, of course; you do have to walk and chew gum at the same time. But you don't differentiate on the basis of those traits. You differentiate on your Missionary DNA.

Alignment, Alignment, Alignment

How do you avoid making a mistake? How do you avoid labeling yourself a Mother, for example, when you're not? Simple. Start by having everyone on your management team take the following DNA test. Then gather everyone together and take a long, hard Spock-like look at the answers—and at your company. Although the ultimate goal of marketing is, of course, a Kirk-like emotional response to a corporate identity—"Just Do It" appeals to the aspirational athlete whether or not those Nike trail shoes will ever traverse terrain any more challenging than the supermarket aisle, whereas Apple's "Think Different" flatters our inner maverick—the first step of the journey must be all Spock: a logical analysis of a company's core DNA.

As a result, I have one hard and fast rule for working with any company: each and every member of the C-suite must participate in the DNA exercise. Remember that determining your company's DNA type and going on to develop a competitive position is not just a marketing exercise with the CMO and the marketing department the only ones involved. Not by a long shot. Pinpointing your company's unique and ideal position in the market reflects that company's business strategy and therefore never should be done in a vacuum. That means everyone from the CEO to the CFO to the CTO to the head of human resources (HR) should be in the room to discuss his or her answers to the test—answers that will serve as a quick and telling indicator of whether the leadership team is on the same page in its idea of and vision for the company. After all, alignment starts with knowing where you're not aligned. (In fact, the leadership team needs to remain involved for the entirety of the positioning exercise.)

Team cohesion is the first step in getting to aha! It is also the first step toward successful implementation of your business and marketing strategies because if there is no alignment within the C-suite, there can be no alignment throughout the company and thus out in the world. So, taking the test individually and then pulling your answers together to see how they line up and where they don't—where the surprises are—is very powerful. It gives you an opportunity to look at the results and say, "Huh? Who answered that one? What's going on here and why?" And it ultimately provides the foundation for a discussion about alignment that all companies need and very few have.

THE DNA TEST

The following 12-question survey will help you identify your company's DNA. From what you've read so far, you may already have a sense of what that DNA is. If that is the case, do your best to push that conviction aside for as long as it takes to complete the test. Remember, it isn't unusual for a company to be convinced of its DNA only to discover after a closer look that the way it sees itself and what it truly is are two very different things.

Keep in mind that this is not a survey about what you *wish* were true about your company. It's about what you *believe is true now* about your company. Without overthinking it, choose for each question the *one* response that best fits your company *as it exists today*.

1. **Which of these statements best describes what your company does?**

   a. We solve a valuable customer need, and we do it better than anyone else.

   b. We build a truly differentiated product with a great value proposition.

   c. We shake things up; our goal is to change the world.

(Continues)

2. **Think about the achievements your company values. Which of these three important achievements do you perceive your company values the most?**

   a. The quality and value of our relationships with customers

   b. Growth in revenue, sales, and adoption of our product

   c. Sparking a movement that changes people's minds or behavior

3. **Which of these three styles of innovation do you believe occurs most naturally at your company?**

   a. Outside-in: What improves the experiences or better solves the needs of a customer or group of customers?

   b. Inside-out: How can we do something better, faster, cheaper?

   c. Way out there: What lies beyond the horizon? What bold idea is next?

4. **Which of these best describes your typical pricing strategy?**

   a. Based on usage or service

   b. Value or cost-plus

   c. Freemium or aspirational

5. **You've just been given a dollar to spend on marketing. On which of the following three projects would your company be most likely to spend that dollar?**

   a. Insight into customer needs and desires

   b. R&D on a truly amazing new product design or feature concept

   c. A thought leadership platform

6. **Which of these three types of people would fit in best with your company culture today?**

   a. Empathetic servant-leaders who intimately know and understand the customers' point of view

   b. Brilliant developers, engineers, and leaders who get things done

   c. Big thinkers who make a "lifestyle choice" by joining our company

7. **Which of these best describes where product marketing resides within your organization today? (If you don't have a formal product marketing organization, check the option for where it most likely would reside if it did exist.)**

   a. Reporting to our CMO—aligned with sales, marketing, operations, and product management

   b. Reporting to our CTO—aligned with product management, IT, and R&D

   c. In the C-suite, reporting to our CEO

8. **For which of the following things is your company's CEO most likely to be lauded in the marketplace?**

   a. Reputation building—for service, relationships, communications, and/or customer experience

   b. Product evolution—for business performance, technical skills, patents, and IP and/or sales achievements

   c. Vision—for gregariousness, personality, inventiveness, pioneering, and/or giant thinking

(Continues)

9. **Which of the following three project proposals would most likely be funded by your executive team at its next meeting?**

   a. An end-to-end target customer experience assessment and redesign canvassing all touchpoints

   b. An R&D project to develop a near-term to medium-term solution to a present or emerging technical problem

   c. A feasibility study on an exciting but theoretical concept

10. **How would your company's leadership team most likely confirm that a value proposition for your company is "correct"?**

   a. We tested it at our latest round of customer advisory groups, and they loved it.

   b. Sales are up, and brand reputation is high. The metrics show it's working.

   c. We simply "feel" it; customers don't know what they want until we invent it.

11. **Which of the following three statements best describes how your company defines the word *brand*?**

   a. The sum of all the experiences a customer has with our company across every touchpoint

   b. The look and feel of our company—our logo, product names, taglines, product packaging, design style, tone of voice, and so on

   c. The way our spirit is embodied—a challenge to the world to think differently

Okay, that's it for the DNA assessment. Just one final question:

12. **Which statement feels most true?**

    a. Answering the questions was easy.

    b. Answering the questions was difficult.

    c. Our management team answered them all differently.

DNA Results

You might have detected a theme here:

- If your answers to the first 11 questions were predominantly (a), you're a Mother.

- If your answers were predominantly (b), you're a Mechanic.

- If your answers were predominantly (c), you're a Missionary.

Assuming that your management team is well aligned, your answers should be fairly consistent. If, for example, eight answers point to you as a Mother, chances are that you truly are a Mother with scattered bits of Mechanic or Missionary DNA sprinkled throughout your genetic background. You now know your DNA type and can begin to focus on identifying or determining your genotype, and it's this next step in corporate DNA analysis that will bring you closer to the aha! positioning you seek. Before you do, however, take some time to look at your results and iron out any differences in opinion about what makes your company tick. The more cohesive you are as a group, the stronger your company's overall alignment and ultimate message will be. Don't be surprised if this little exercise sparks some hard-core emotion. Get it on the table, dissect it, and determine where the differences lie. Not only will this be time well spent in creating a cohesive management team, it will make marketing easier.

What do you do, however, when your answers are less definitive? Many companies tally their group results and even after extensive discussion find they come out pretty evenly split between two DNA types. Although that initially may seem an intractable problem, it's not. Just as my green eyes tell you I have the genetic material for both brown eyes and blue eyes in my DNA background, some companies are a mix of two different genetic types. Once that becomes clear, it's up to the management team to decide which genetic type is to be the facing personality. And once that decision has been made, those promoting other DNA types will have to give up the ghost and adopt the dominant DNA. For example, I worked with Hector Ruiz when he led the semiconductor division at Motorola and then again when he was CEO of AMD. He had a great philosophy on this topic that I have come to call the Hector Ruiz Principle: "We build consensus by getting 60 percent of the management team to agree on a direction and 100 percent of them to buy in on that direction." That's the type of leadership that encourages alignment.

Don't forget: your background DNA won't disappear. In fact, it is likely to show up in certain aspects of your product or service, such as with Steve Jobs's determination that Apple be user-friendly as well as conceptually groundbreaking, and it will become a pillar supporting the dominant DNA. In the end, there can be only one DNA type and one genotype (strategic direction) within that DNA type to ensure that the gears turn with the least amount of friction.

The whole idea behind identifying your DNA is to avoid sending your product or service into a competitive arena that is out of concert with your genetic makeup, thus making it more difficult for you to succeed. After all, good athletes compete to win by attempting to be the very best they can be given who they are at their core. Everything else is an improvement on that.

Let's say that after a great deal of discussion about your team's answers, you still find your company planted firmly between Mechanic and Missionary: maybe five answers point to Mechanic, five to Missionary, and one to Mother. That actually gives you some wiggle room in terms of which category you choose, but you'll ultimately have to apply the Hector Ruiz Principle to relieve the tension. In point of fact, the DNA test is more diagnostic than prescriptive. If you market yourself as a Mechanic, you'll probably do okay. If you opt instead to position as a Missionary, you'll also probably do okay, assuming you create consensus within the leadership team and co-opt any stragglers. But if you decide you want to position as a Mother because you've bought into the customer-centric rhetoric, your campaign will be completely out of whack with your genetic makeup, and that's a problem. Now you're a five-foot three-inch guy who wants to play basketball with the Golden State Warriors because you have the ability to be a team player.

Consider Comcast, a Features-focused Mechanic notorious for customer service that is considered so awful that the company has been the butt of jokes for years. Now, however, Comcast is trying to turn its image around. It's trying to shift its DNA by revamping its website and initiating a new customer-friendly advertising campaign. But is Comcast simply a wolf in sheep's clothing? Is it trying to be perceived as a customer-centric company by making all the right adjustments to its language and customer service contact points but without making any real changes to its core DNA? Important questions to consider: Has Comcast revamped its leadership by hiring more Mothers? Has it changed its compensation programs to reflect customer priority? Is it measuring success with a Net Promoter Score? Or, more likely, is the company just putting lipstick on a pig? As we'll see in Chapter 7, changing DNA isn't easy or cheap. As a result, a more cost-effective way for Comcast to improve its public image might be to forget about trying to be a Mother and instead accentuate its Mechanic status by marketing (and of course making) its products and features better than the competition's, an effort that wouldn't require much in the way of customer service.

The outcome of the DNA test will guide you toward the positioning approach that will work in concert with who you are as a company. At the same time, it will help steer you away from approaches that are out of concert with who you are. If you land squarely as a Missionary, for example, you now know that there are two directions for you to go in the market: you can shoot for the Next Big Thing or you can focus on Cult of Personality. Both work with your DNA, and you can let the others go. If you come up straddling Mothers and Missionaries, however, you know that the only directions you can toss aside for now—until you come to a firm agreement as a team on which face to present to the world—are the two Mechanic genotypes: Value and Features.

This is important whether you are a long-standing team or a brand-new one that has never had the opportunity to jell around a specific corporate DNA type. New teams have to assess where their individual members reside on the spectrum and apply the Hector Ruiz Principle to a decision, which should be made by the CEO, the team's strategic leader: 60 percent agreement, 100 percent buy-in.

As for the last question—the one about how easy or difficult it was to answer the test—your answers can tell you a great deal about alignment among your leadership team. If you find your organization is split down the middle—5 people felt that the company's DNA type was Mother, and 5 leaned toward Mechanic—and 9 out of 10 reported that the test was difficult to complete, that's a big red flag. If you're not sure how to answer individually, let alone as a group, you've got a lot to sort out in terms of strategy and communication. Similarly, if the test was easy for everyone—the answers seemed obvious—but the results are still split, with everyone landing on a different DNA type, that's a serious issue as well. Either way, it tells you that you have a lot to hash out as a management team.

On the flip side, if your team is well aligned—the answers to the DNA test were definitive—and most people found the questions easy to answer, the last question can serve as a confidence booster as you turn your attention to exactly how to market your company's product or service. If the C-suite is well aligned but nearly everyone reported that coming up with the answers was a struggle, the results can serve to put individual concerns to rest. That's good news: once your team is on the same DNA page and has taken the genotype test that follows, the hardest part of determining how to position your company for maximum competitive advantage is behind you.

THE GENOTYPE TEST

DNA Type: Mother, Genotype: Customer Experience

- Is your company maniacal about the experience your customers have with you?
  - ❑ Yes
  - ❑ No

- Does your company covet a high Net Promoter Score?
  - ❑ Yes
  - ❑ No

- Does your company talk incessantly about delighting your customers?
  - ❑ Yes
  - ❑ No

(Continues)

- Does your company tell stories about customers in most meetings?
  - ❏ Yes
  - ❏ No

If you've answered yes to at least three of these four questions, your Mother genotype is Customer Experience.

DNA Type: Mother, Genotype: Customer Segmentation

- Does your company focus intently on customer segmentation?
  - ❏ Yes
  - ❏ No

- Can you pinpoint the customer segments your company addresses?
  - ❏ Yes
  - ❏ No

- Are those customer segments easily identified by age, gender, job, activity, or aspiration?
  - ❏ Yes
  - ❏ No

- Does your company refer to its customers with any sort of affectionate or unique name?
  - ❏ Yes
  - ❏ No

If you've answered yes to at least three of these four questions, your Mother genotype is Customer Segmentation.

DNA Type: Mechanic, Genotype: Value

- Are you a commodity product or service?
  - ❑ Yes
  - ❑ No

- Does your company focus on more for less in its messaging?
  - ❑ Yes
  - ❑ No

- Does your company promote itself as a provider of a product or service that offers a rare value in your industry?
  - ❑ Yes
  - ❑ No

- Do you frequently compare your prices with those of your competitors in management meetings?
  - ❑ Yes
  - ❑ No

If you've answered yes to at least three of these four questions, your Mechanic genotype is Value.

DNA Type: Mechanic, Genotype: Features

- Does your company introduce new features several times a year with at least some fanfare?
  - ❑ Yes
  - ❑ No

- Do you talk a lot about competitive-feature comparison in management meetings?
  - ❑ Yes
  - ❑ No

(Continues)

- Does your company focus on the intricacies of its product in its messaging?
  - ❑ Yes
  - ❑ No

- Does your company participate in feature-by-feature third-party competitive testing?
  - ❑ Yes
  - ❑ No

If you've answered yes to at least three of these four questions, your Mechanic genotype is Features.

DNA Type: Missionary, Genotype: Next Big Thing

- Is your company changing behavior in its market?
  - ❑ Yes
  - ❑ No

- Is your product or service redefining an industry or creating a new one?
  - ❑ Yes
  - ❑ No

- Are your customers primarily "early adopters"?
  - ❑ Yes
  - ❑ No

- Does your company eschew market research?
  - ❑ Yes
  - ❑ No

If you've answered yes to at least three of these four questions, your Missionary genotype is Next Big Thing.

DNA Type: Missionary, Genotype: Cult of Personality

- Does your company have an extremely charismatic CEO or product?
  - ☐ Yes
  - ☐ No

- Do people come to work at your company as a lifestyle choice?
  - ☐ Yes
  - ☐ No

- Are customers and industry influencers aware of your corporate culture and able to define it?
  - ☐ Yes
  - ☐ No

- Is cultural fit a primary criterion for hiring?
  - ☐ Yes
  - ☐ No

If you've answered yes to at least three of these four questions, your Missionary genotype is Cult of Personality.

Now you know that you're a Mechanic with a Features genotype. Or a Mother with a Customer Experience genotype. Or maybe you're a Missionary with a Cult of Personality genotype. What's important is that you have a pretty good idea of who and what you are. Now it's time to apply that knowledge to the rest of the positioning process.

4

The Six Cs of Positioning

lthough the genetic type is the single biggest factor in positioning, DNA is not the only consideration; there are other elements—the environment—that go into determining a company's ideal position in the market landscape. When my team and I work with clients to develop positioning, we take a close look at them and their ecosystems through six distinct lenses: Core (the company DNA), Category, Community, Competition, Context, and Criteria (Figure 4.1).

Any marketing campaign worth its salt takes into account Category, Community, Competition, and Context. The framework outlined in this book, however, is the only one that introduces two new Cs: Core DNA at the front end and Criteria for positioning at the back end. Once Core DNA has been discovered, the role of the remaining Cs is to illuminate the opportunities inherent in a company's genetic disposition. In turn, Core DNA offers a guiding light for pinpointing the other Cs. In essence, each is affected by the company's DNA, and vice versa. Adding Criteria to the process helps us define what we want the positioning to include and gives us a checklist at the end of the exercise to ensure that we've hit the nail on the head.

FIGURE 4.1 Positioning Assessment Framework

Core was covered in detail in Chapter 3. Descriptions of the other five Cs follow.

To what grouping of like companies does yours belong?

Category

Where does your company fit within the market landscape? Is there a particular category you can claim with your product or service? Does your company fit into any category at all? Or are you creating a new category? Redefining an existing one? No matter your goal, the category you choose sets the boundaries for the landscape in which you intend to compete. It also shapes the world's understanding of the company you intend to keep, that is, who your competitors are. Although nearly every marketing consulting firm considers Category when it is preparing a marketing plan, the framework outlined here addresses Category as a multisided strategy decision.

There is no question that changing human behavior, as Steve Jobs did time and again, can be fun and exciting, and for that reason Missionaries often are seen as "cool" category builders. As a result, nearly everyone wants to be one. But you don't have to be a Missionary to build a category or a subcategory. You do, however, have to be careful about the decision to do this. Creating categories is a tricky business; true category creation takes a great deal of time, effort, and money, not to mention consideration of a slew of other companies that are or will become competitors in your new category. After all, there is no such thing as a category of one.

Although many new categories are created by Missionaries—Salesforce, for example, redefined software as a service delivered in the cloud—it's important to understand (and repeat) that you do *not* have to be a Missionary to create a new one. Established Mothers and Mechanics are fully capable of creating new categories—or, more often, subcategories—either on their own, as Avaya, a Mechanic, did with customer and team "engagement," or by buying and absorbing a company, just as Oracle, another Mechanic, did when it beat out rival SAP to acquire retail software company (and fellow Mechanic) Retek to create "empowered commerce."

Being a Missionary does not automatically equate to category creation. Take Tesla, for example. Although it certainly will be remembered as an industry game changer for its success in creating a battery powerful enough to combat range anxiety, Tesla is not a category creator. After all, electric cars have been around for a hundred years. Elon Musk just took them to the next level. He refined them and in doing so became a category refiner. (Even before the first car rolled off the factory floor, Tesla's "entry-level" Model 3 helped push the company further along the technological adoption curve.)

As Steve Jobs famously said, "Good artists copy, great artists steal." Some of the best categories were created by pioneers who were eclipsed by the second or third or tenth player in the market who figured out how to make the category a success—who essentially figured out how to steal the best parts of the pioneer's progress and take it from there. These are the companies that go down in history as the category creators, not the ones that developed the category or the category name in the first place.

If you think from a technology perspective about some of the most innovative categories in the world today, you'll notice that they are made up of once-disparate words—generic words—that were pulled together to characterize something new: *telephone, television, airplane, airline, personal computer, desktop publishing, cloud computing, domestic robot*, and so on. History tells us that Alexander Graham Bell invented the telephone, that IBM developed the first personal computer, that the Wright brothers came up with the first airplane, and that Aldus Corporation (later acquired by Adobe) developed desktop publishing. But each category became a category only when other companies developed competitive products and in so doing launched a new industry. That's when the stealing begins. Individual inventors may or may not receive their due in the historical record, but either way, category creation does not pay off until there are several companies building competitive products.

In light of such challenges, disrupting from within a known category to create a subcategory is an alternative to outright category creation. As evidenced by the innumerable array of beverage categories (sodas, diet sodas, caffeine-free sodas, fizzy drinks, juice drinks, vitamin water, light beer, and craft beer, to name just a few), food options (organic, fat free, gluten free, salt free, vegan, and artisanal, among many more), and vehicle models (SUVs, minivans, pickup trucks, tiny cars, hybrids, electric vehicles, etc.), there is a vast world of subcategories waiting to be invented and launched.

When it comes to subcategories, consumers often don't even know what they want until it's offered. For example, somebody toiling away at Chrysler some 30-odd years ago came up with the idea of building a fuel-efficient family vehicle that drove like a car; was well suited for transporting a lot of passengers; had plenty of space for sports equipment, camping gear, and other cargo; and featured a sliding door to make it easier to load kids in and out of the back. Voilà! The minivan was born (a birth, by the way, that saved Chrysler from extinction). Later, someone else thought, Hey, how about a sliding door on both sides? Wouldn't that be even better? And so on. Adaptations and features are about making money and beating out the competition, but they're also grounded in someone doing the homework to figure out what is best for the customer, someone who asks: "What pain point does this solve, and who might buy it?"

That's how subcategories are created. It's all a matter of building a customized solution for a group of people: Amazon redefined the IT outsourcing model with Amazon Web Services. Squarespace took web publishing and made it do-it-yourself. Marketo popularized automation software in the marketing community. Etsy created a personal, creative marketplace within the larger online shopping community.

One company I have really enjoyed working with in this context over the years is Sitecore. A Mechanic known for content management software, Sitecore wanted to be a leader in the "customer experience management" category. But while customer experience management will likely become a viable marketing category in a few years, it hadn't yet been well defined, and our research showed that no one really understood what it meant. After talking with one of the company's senior tech people, however, it became clear that everything Sitecore does is geared toward giving clients the ability to market in a certain context—to personalize content down to the individual. Bam! That was the aha! Instead of working to establish a presence in a category that as yet remains undefined, why not aim instead to become the leader in the subcategory of "context marketing," a term that has been generating buzz in the industry over the past couple of years, but that no one had yet settled on, much less owned? Context marketing is exactly what Sitecore does, and since people were already talking about it, the company could adopt the term without worrying about it being too vague, and without the danger of becoming a category of one. The result? Sitecore is now the leader in context marketing. The company was able to grab a phrase that was already in use in an existing category and claim it for its own.

In addition to helping companies develop new categories and subcategories, I have spent a great deal of time working with other firms to tweak and expand existing categories. Because creating a category is expensive and time-consuming and often doesn't work out as planned (the history of flying cars in the twentieth century, for example, is filled with more crashes than flights, though that history is likely to be rewritten in the near future), companies also can consider redefining a category, an idea that is very much in keeping with the message outlined in W. Chan Kim and Renée Mauborgne's *Blue Ocean Strategy*. In fact, redefining a category is exactly what Amazon did in 1994 by announcing in essence, "We're just like Borders, only online." It's a lot easier to get consumer mindshare when you're redefining something everyone already understands than it is to open up white space for a product no one can yet fathom. That's why new companies attempting to capitalize on other companies' successes often use the model company in their positioning statements: "We're the McDonald's of XYZ" or "We're the Uber of ABC."

The key to redefining a category is seeing possibility where others don't. That is what Brian Chesky, founder and CEO of Airbnb, did when he thought about how many empty couches around the world could be turned into inexpensive beds for travelers, particularly in destinations where lodging was both scarce and pricey. Over time those budget couches became beds, then rooms, and eventually apartments and homes—even camping trailers. Chesky didn't create the home-sharing model—VRBO and HomeAway came first—but he certainly refined it. Airbnb's positioning was about the couch, not the house, at least initially. It repositioned the category to serve a lower-end customer—one who wanted a couch, not a house—and a new industry was born.

The beauty of Airbnb is that at its best, you feel embraced and cared for. The company has the home-away-from-home concept down pat; that is not surprising given its Mother status. Even compared with other home-sharing services, Airbnb offers a casual yet intimate element, one where you might get to meet the owner and shake hands. That's very different from the impersonal nature of a roadside motel or large chain hotel. Although founded in 2008, Airbnb has completely upended the hotel industry—changing travel behavior along the way—and today is valued higher than hotel giant Marriott International, pulling in between $500 million and $1 billion a year. The company also led Glassdoor's annual "50 Best Places to Work" roster in 2016, taking the overall top spot, toppling Google as the best tech company to work for in the United States.

Sometimes companies try to redefine themselves by switching categories. An example is BlackBerry, a Mechanic in the smartphone category that was all but given up for dead by many. The company, which is a client of ours, is currently reviving its brand by expanding beyond devices and establishing itself as a leader in the enterprise software and security realm. After reviewing BlackBerry's assets, turnaround CEO John Chen launched a pivot strategy of moving from hardware to software, an example of a company shifting its Mechanic DNA from Features to Value. The company has made great progress in this endeavor by staking an ownership position in a new space—the Enterprise of Things—and by declaring its mission to secure it. Thus its new positioning statement: "BlackBerry is pivoting to leverage its leadership in security and mobility to secure, connect, and mobilize the enterprise by connecting people, devices, processes, and systems and in so doing, fully realize a secure Enterprise of Things." Market traction is taking hold, and even the analyst community is lauding the company's new position.

In today's fast-moving economy, categories can change in an instant, and any category you join, create, or reframe may look completely different in a month or a year—or even next week—so be judicious with your category choice. It's exciting to create a category, but it's even more exciting to see your company scale. Choose your category because it's *right*, not because it's exciting. Case in point: when

Bezos launched Amazon, he positioned the company as an "online bookseller," placing it squarely in the same category as Barnes & Noble, Borders, and other brick-and-mortar bookstores. He knew that to get traction, he needed to disrupt from within a known category.

Whatever classification you ultimately determine, be prepared to thrive in a category of many. As I have said, there really is no such thing as a category of one, at least not for very long. Even if you have no direct competitors (yet), your customers do have alternatives for solving their problems. And if your space is truly promising, players in tangential categories are soon to follow you there—if they aren't already on track to do exactly that. Choose a category that you can own now and in the near future.

Who are your stakeholders and what are their needs?

Community

Although there are many elements to Category, the next C, Community, is far more straightforward though no less important. Why? Because whatever position in the marketing landscape you choose, that position must solve a need of a large and sustainable population. Your customer is your most valuable stakeholder, one with biases, behaviors, and beliefs that matter. And that customer is surrounded by influencers, each a part of your community as well.

Just knowing who your customers are—new moms, neurosurgeons, network engineers—is not enough. You also need to know why they care about what you have to offer and understand why it's relevant to them. You need to find out how they learn about solutions such as yours. Who influences their buying decisions? Who are the other actors that appear in the buying cycle? In some cases, your innovation may be transformative enough that potential customers or their influencers won't be able to tell you anything; in fact, they may not even realize they have a problem you're able to solve. (Who knew sliding doors would make minivans so popular with parents? Or that there was such a large market for a one-touch online car service until Uber hit the streets?) Even so, your customers speak a distinct language; they are driven by specific motivations and influenced by a variety of factors, all of which must be taken into consideration during the positioning process.

It is often obvious who your customers are or might be, but identifying the circle of influence that surrounds them may take some sleuthing. Product reviews, press coverage, the blogosphere, social media, and analyst reports are typical sources of influence, but depending on the product, there are likely to be still more. In the healthcare industry, doctors, chiropractors, nurses, and insurance companies are influencers. In the sporting goods industry, athletes and their fan bases are influencers. In the security industry, academics, consultants, cybersecurity experts, and government officials are influencers. Whatever the field, influencers are many and varied, and it pays to discover and then market to them as well as to potential customers.

The circle of influence is known as your target audience. Your target market is the sea of people to whom you want to sell your product, and the best way to tackle it is to segment or profile it. For example, Snap-on, which manufactures high-end tools, diagnostics, equipment, software, and service solutions, is a great example of a company that knows to concentrate its marketing efforts on mechanics and building professionals (and the publications they read). The company also knows that if it sends Snap-on trucks out to job sites where there are a whole bunch of mechanics and building professionals, it has a good shot at both reinforcing the brand (via the truck's logo) and selling tools on the spot. Good marketing, right? But it gets even better. The company understands that those buyers can act as influencers. After buying tools from a Snap-on truck, those mechanics and building profession-als return to the job site, where they show off their new purchases to their coworkers. Those workers may be inclined to head out to the truck to see for themselves what they can buy. This is a brilliant marketing strategy that reinforces the brand, creates a ripple effect, and sells prod-uct. The company is successful because it understands its customer and what influences that customer. Snap-on doesn't spend a lot of time or money chasing the weekend hammer-and-wrench set; it knows it doesn't need to. Professional mechanics and builders aspire to use pro-fessional tools, and so they actually seek out Snap-on as a brand to buy.

Similarly, though Ford and Ferrari are both out to woo buyers eager and able to purchase a car, they know to isolate their target mar-ket on the basis of who is willing to spend upward of $400,000 on a car and who isn't. Ford (a Mother) knows how to appeal to Everyman, and Ferrari (a Mechanic) knows how to appeal to the luxury set. Their posi-tioning, and thus their marketing, are completely aligned. DNA-based positioning helps them further align their marketing with the authen-ticity of the brand. When it comes to segmenting customers, the goal is to pinpoint your exact market as closely as possible and then learn how to reach those customers. Where do they hang out? Where do they live? What conferences and events do they attend? What do they read? What do they watch on TV? What social media do they use?

If you had to choose one and only one core customer for whom you exist, could you do that easily? Would all your team members answer the same way? If that is not the case, you have work to do. You can never be all things to all people (and to make that your goal is a recipe for failure), but *someone* is representative of your primary cus-tomer. Position your company to appeal to that particular someone. Also make sure that such positioning is appropriate for your custom-ers' circles of influence. Because when you position for a particular and segmented customer base, you are also positioning for the circle of influence that surrounds that segment. You are tapping into an eco-system with a clear and coherent message.

Who are your competitors?

Competition

When it comes to your competition, great positioning is informed by the strengths and weaknesses of the alternatives to your product or service as well as by what is going on within your ecosystem. When you are staking a claim in a category that you feel you can own and win, expect the landscape to change around you and to change quickly. The better you understand and predict your evolving alternatives, the better you can evolve your own position and the more leeway you'll have to shape the category rather than have it shaped for you. In considering the competition, I like to use two visual tools to gain mastery over the situation: the standard XY axes diagram and Steve Blank's petal diagram. Not only do these visuals compel your team to consider the obvious competitors in the obvious categories, they also highlight the white space, identify potential attackers, and consider tangential categories from which other entrants might encroach.

The XY Diagram

I suggest creating a classic XY diagram to see where your company stands in comparison to the competition. Start by compiling a list of the considerations most critical to your customers (another reason to know exactly who you are selling to and what they care about). Possibilities include price, ease of use, completeness of solution, and ability to integrate with other tangential products. Choose one—price, for example—and make that the X axis, with "Inexpensive" at the far left and "Expensive" at the far right. Pick a second—ability to integrate with other tangential products, perhaps—and map it along the Y axis, with "Low Ability" at the bottom and "High Ability" at the top. Next, place your competitors within the diagram, including as many as you can. When you're done, pinpoint the spot where you think your company belongs. In addition to providing a visual reference to how crowded your market is, it will reveal the white spaces, the areas that are available to be owned.

Repeat the exercise with the remaining considerations on your list. By the time you've completed four or five diagrams, you'll have identified the white spaces for all relevant considerations and you'll know where your product could slide in and take ownership. And ownership, of course, is the goal. What is that space that only you can own with your product or service? Equally important, who surrounds you and is threatening to crowd you out or eat your lunch?

Steve Blank's Petal Diagram

To illustrate the importance of expanding perspective and eliminating bias during positioning, consider the Indian parable of the six blind monks and an elephant. Each monk was asked to touch just one part of the elephant and describe what it was in the context of what he felt:

- "It is a sturdy pillar," said the monk who touched only the leg.

- "It is a smooth, hard pipe," said the monk who touched only the tusk.

- "It is a thick tree branch," said the monk who touched only the trunk.

- "It is a coarse rope," said the monk who touched only the tail.

- "It is a broad, thin fan," said the monk who touched only the ear.

- "It is a firm wall," said the monk who touched only the flank.

They were all right, of course. But it was only after combining all of their perspectives that the monks were able to come to a more complete truth about the elephant as a whole.

The beauty of the petal diagram—which can expand to accommodate as many market segments as needed—is that it forces everyone to look at the problem of competitive differentiation from distinct points of view, a wide-angle lens that is particularly useful for startups as well as for companies looking to create new markets (or expand existing ones). Aspects to consider include the language competitors use, the DNA of competitor companies, and the brands with which you might want to align, cooperate, or simply compete, drawing as many adjacent market segments as necessary (Figure 4.2).

This is the kind of analysis that leads to aha! And of course, these visual tools can be used in a variety of ways: to expand competitive

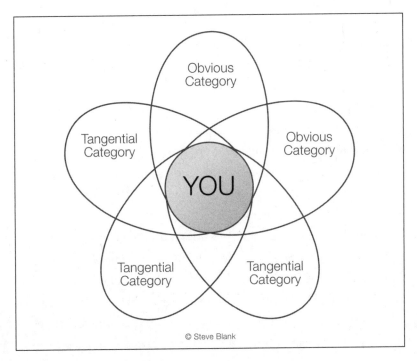

© Steve Blank

FIGURE 4.2 Competitive Landscape

analysis beyond the C-suite and throughout your company's departments, to predict your customers' needs and desires, to evaluate what you want in your next executive hire, and so on. However it's deployed, what's important is that you're looking beyond the traditional and inspecting the competitive landscape as a whole.

What trends and forces are shaping the market?

Context

Equally important in successful positioning is to consider the forces that currently shape the market—and even the world at large. The market landscape is always shifting, and so it is essential to adapt by capitalizing on the trends that influence customer beliefs, behaviors, and language and to incorporate the implications of those trends into your product or service. That is exactly what Jeff Bezos did with Amazon in adapting a mainstream activity—buying books—to the evolving world of online commerce. It's what Nike, the top player in the athletic apparel market, did in pushing beyond basic sports gear to dominate the "athleisure" trend. And it's what Uber did in implementing a one-button car service app that makes the most of consumers' increasing reliance on mobile technology.

Probably the easiest way to ensure that your product or service is positioned with Context in mind is to fall back on one of the following phrases: "We're the Uber of ..." "We're the Facebook of ..." or "We're the Apple of. ..." The rush to "Uberize" services underscores the fact that companies want to capitalize on the success of Uber as well as others in the sharing economy by taking advantage of excess capacity in a specific market. (In light of all the scandals that have emerged at Uber, it's a shame Airbnb and Lyft aren't better verbs.) Where venture capital is concerned, this isn't a bad strategy. The VC community knows how successful Uber has been (scandals aside), it knows the model is hot, and it knows that it can be applied to many different things. The strategy may work for customers as well. But as I have discovered firsthand over the last several months working as an advisor to a company that is "Uberizing warehouse capacity," an oversimplification of positioning can thwart any marketing effort. The complexities involved in Uberizing this particular B2B business, which is heavily dependent on multiple IT systems coming together and tracking goods from place to place, make it a far cry from what Travis Kalanick faced when he gathered drivers and deployed them and their cars for on-demand passenger rides.

As I write this book, there is so much more happening in our world to which we can relate, so many waves we can ride for positioning purposes. Artificial intelligence and machine learning offer opportunities to position products and services as "smart." The cloud computing trend enables us to capitalize on the cloud in positioning statements. Social media provide a plethora of possibilities for introducing social products or services. Virtual and augmented reality are hot, as are robotics, consumer healthcare, localization, cybersecurity, and analytics for just about everything. Not to mention trends outside of technology such as globalization, millennial culture, microfinancing, angel investing, the tidy-up movement, and the cocktails craze, among so many others. The point here is that your positioning statement must be relevant, and it must resonate in the context in which you will use it to market and sell your product or service.

To illustrate this point, TechCrunch's article on "10 of the coolest gadgets we saw at CES 2017" offers a compendium of new product launches positioned to ride a number of current waves. All are consumer gadgets, but gadgets have to be positioned too, and their marketers did a pretty good job of that. As is summarized below, they provide great examples of positioning with context in mind:

- Plume is a pollution-tracking wearable positioned as a "Fitbit for air quality." Designed for people who live in big polluted cities, the device, which also can be clipped to a bag, measures particulate matter, nitrogen dioxide, ozone, volatile organic compounds, temperature, and humidity.

- The Griffin Connected Toaster is positioned as a smart toaster that lets you define exactly how much to toast your bagel or English muffin. The app features a slider with an icon of a white piece of bread on one side and a black one on the other. As TechCrunch notes, "Sure, a smart toaster is the epitome of connected appliance ridiculousness, but there's something to be said for being able to micromanage the level of bread toastedness to such a microscopic level."

- Milo Sensors showcased Proof, a wearable positioned as a discreet breathalyzer. While noting that "Checking your blood alcohol content with a breathalyzer while out with some friends might just be a party trick," TechCrunch acknowledges that if you really want to know whether to have another drink, "it might be awkward to pull one out." The company's sensor, worn as a small band, detects various chemicals in the wearer's perspiration—information that is transmitted to the app—allowing users to monitor their blood alcohol levels continually just by checking their phones.

- Kuri is positioned as an adorable robotic home companion and assistant. Just 20 inches tall and weighing 14 pounds, she features blinking eyes, a swiveling head, a cute round form, lights, and beeping noises. Similar to Google Home and Amazon Echo and Alexa, Kuri responds to verbal input and operates as a voice command–activated security camera.

- Positioned as a wearable that monitors fitness and sleep, Motiv's tracking device "has crammed a whole fitness band's worth of functionality into a ring," according to TechCrunch. In addition to measuring sleep, steps, distance, and calories, the ring, which is encased in titanium, features a heart rate sensor. Its battery lasts three to five days on one charge.

- Best known for making smart glasses for the military, the Osterhout Design Group showcased its first consumer augmented reality/virtual reality glasses, which it is positioning as "smart glasses to the masses." According to the company, the glasses—which are powered by Qualcomm's Snapdragon 835 chip—"play movies with cinematic clarity, drop you inside immersive 3D interactive experiences, and reveal new worlds of invention and productivity."

- Positioned as a pairing of nostalgia and the latest in high-tech photography, the Polaroid Pop revisits Polaroid's iconic instant format with its latest offering, a three- by four-inch photo-printing camera. As a follow-up to the successful smaller Snap camera, the rear of the device features a touchscreen LCD, allowing users to see their shots before they're developed. The verdict? TechCrunch reports that the prints "look pretty great."

- Clear Flight Solutions' Robird is a drone that, as TechCrunch says, "scares the bejesus out of other birds to keep aviation safe." Positioned as a creative way to combat the threat of bird strikes around airports, the drone is designed to mimic a raptor and "flies by flapping its wings and steers by using two tail fins. It can even glide through the air for periods of time, just like a stalking bird of prey would do."

- The Willow breast pump enables hands-free mobile pumping. Positioned as a wearable that offers breast-feeding mothers liberation from the drudgery of being stuck in one place while expressing milk, the cordless Willow—which contains sealed single-use plastic bags—slips inside a nursing bra and detects when a woman's milk begins to flow, adjusting the pump mode automatically. It also pairs with an app to track pumping time and volume.

- Although there was a veritable sea of TVs at CES, Sony's XBR-A1E Bravia 4K OLED, complete with Dolby Vision HDR, managed to catch TechCrunch's attention. The only acronym that matters here is OLED (Organic Light Emitting Diode), a type of display technology that makes it possible to build TVs that are even slimmer than the slimmest LCD or plasma sets. According to Sony, OLED facilitates "unprecedented black levels, rich and lifelike color, dynamic contrast, blur-less image, and a wide viewing angle." Positioned as the latest thing in all-in-one television, the Sony device has an edge-to-edge design and sits directly on the ground or a table and leans against a back stand that houses the TV's processor and other essential parts. The design also means there are no speakers surrounding the TV. Instead, technology Sony calls Acoustic Surface enables the sound to come from the screen itself.

What is required to make your positioning statement successful?

Criteria

Unlike the other Cs, which grow out of the environment, Criteria is a set of parameters that should come from the team after it has examined the other five Cs. It should be the last step you take before developing the actual positioning statement. The trick here is to compile a list of five to seven factors you want your positioning statement to accomplish so that you'll know you've arrived when you're there. For example, a retail company eager to appeal to millennials might include among its Criteria the following elements: hipness, 24/7 accessibility, value-based offers, sustainability, and philanthropy. As with every aspect of the positioning exercise, Criteria requires agreement across the C-suite, since the resulting statement must be embraced by the team. Each member will bring different Criteria to the table to be judged, and so it's important to have everyone articulate what is true on an individual level and then agree as a group. The better a team of executives can articulate and align on Criteria ahead of time, the easier it is for them to arrive at positioning they collectively trust and can embrace. Decide on your Criteria and expect to hit about 75 percent of them in the final positioning statement. After all, you can never be all things to all people. Pick the most important ones and shoot for simplicity over inclusion.

Superpower Strength

Understanding what you have to offer and knowing to whom are critical to positioning, but they are only segments of the marketing equation as a whole. Before you can go there, much less begin to tackle your brand, you must first understand who you are at your genetic core. This is why I always start with the DNA exercise. At the same time, it's important to realize that although Core is a critical addition to the other Cs, each is crucial to determining a company's role and relevance, and to skip one would be like baking a cake and leaving out sugar or flour. But Core is the magic ingredient that makes the cake special. Or, to switch food metaphors, it is the special sauce that makes a Big Mac a Big Mac. Here lies the magic of the method, its superpower strength.

Not surprisingly then, most of the time it's Core DNA that paves the way for positioning. But not always. Sometimes, one of the other Cs will take the lead-dog position and a company's positioning strategy will grow out of that instead. Category or Context are examples; either of them might have been the case with Amazon's launch, given my belief that Bezos was aware of the potential inherent in online shopping and had his eye on the bulk of the iceberg lying beneath the e-commerce waterline. Even so, had Amazon tried to position from day one as anything other than a Missionary determined to transform the world of books and commerce, it probably would have hit a roadblock (although as we'll see in Chapter 7, Amazon has undergone a DNA change and today operates as a Mother). When Core DNA is right and your team is aligned—resulting in spot-on positioning—you amplify the impact of marketing. You avoid friction. You accelerate growth. When the answers are misaligned among your team members, however, your path to market will be slower and more difficult.

The final step in getting to aha! is to begin the process of fitting all the Cs together to come up with a positioning statement, something we will explore in Chapter 5.

5

Positioning and
Message Architecture

It's time to get down to brass tacks and begin dealing with the message architecture, which is the single most useful marketing tool in the shed. The critical element of the message architecture is, of course, the positioning statement, which articulates a company's unique role and relevance in the market. Let's start by exploring how to write that statement, beginning with the toughest questions in business: "Who are you?" and "Why do you matter?"

By this stage in the process you've examined the market through the six lenses discussed in the previous chapters: Core, Category, Community, Competition, Context, and Criteria. You know your Core DNA type, the Category in which you intend to play (or build), the Community you are serving and speaking to, the Competition you face, and the Context in which your product exists in the market. You should have developed a list of Criteria for your positioning statement that will help you determine whether you've hit the nail on the head at the end of the exercise. Finally, you know that a positioning statement is a rational, practical, factual statement about your role and relevance.

What Works and What Doesn't

Let's look at a few examples of positioning statements and their corresponding elevator stories (an element of the message architecture addressed later in this chapter) and determine what is good and bad about them. All of the following are acceptable but could be better with some honing. These companies' positioning statements have been embedded in their elevator stories or narratives, which I've retrieved from their websites and copied below (in the case of longer elevator stories, only the sentences focused on positioning are italicized):

- *Mobileye* appears to be a Mechanic with a Features focus:

  - Elevator story: *"Mobileye is the leading supplier of software that enables Advanced Driver Assist Systems (ADAS), with more than 25 automaker partners including some of the world's largest.* Beyond ADAS, our technology has rapidly evolved to also support the three pillars of Autonomous Driving—Sensing, Mapping, and Driving Policy. As a result of this broad and well-advanced product offering, we have achieved a partnership to develop production-ready Fully Autonomous Vehicles with BMW and Intel, with production launch planned for 2021, and another partnership with the Tier-1 supplier Delphi for a 'turnkey' system to be productized starting from 2019 with customer OEMs."

  - Good: Asserts a unique position within a confined market and addresses relevance with the proof point of 25 leading industry partners.

- º Bad: Fails to address the company's uniqueness beyond being the leader, provides no differentiation from competitors, and offers no real value proposition.

- *The Container Store* is clearly a Customer Experience Mother asserting her "devotion" to bringing order to customers surrounded by chaos:

  - º Elevator story: *"We are the original storage and organization specialty retailer and the only national retailer solely devoted to the category. Our goal is to help provide order to an increasingly busy and chaotic world. We provide creative, multifunctional, customizable storage and organization solutions that help our customers save time, save space, and improve the quality of their lives."*

  - º Good: Addresses context through quality of life concerns (helping customers save time and space); in line with the new "clutter-free" movement.

  - º Bad: Fails to explain the "experience" inherent in being a Customer Experience Mother. Also fails to differentiate itself from its competitors other than by asserting that it is the "original storage and organization specialty retailer," which actually doesn't matter to customers.

- *Verizon* appears to be in the middle of a genetic makeover, moving from a Value Mechanic to a Customer Experience Mother:

  - º Elevator story: *"We help people, businesses and things communicate better.* The digital world promises consumers a better, more connected life, and we're the ones delivering it. *We make it possible for people to stay in touch and businesses to connect with their customers.* We're also bringing technology and hands-on learning opportunities directly to kids who need it most. Our goal is to inspire tomorrow's creators to use technology to build brighter futures for themselves, their families and the world."

    ○ Good: Asserts a value proposition and answers two key questions: "Why Verizon?" and "Why now?"

    ○ Bad: Fails to differentiate or explain what the Verizon experience actually is, describing it simply as "better" (which says nothing).

- *Logitech* is another Customer Experience Mother:

    ○ Elevator story (this one is a long one, and the architect would have had to add several floors to a building to accommodate it): "Focused on innovation and quality, *Logitech designs personal peripherals to help people enjoy a better experience with the digital world.* We started in 1981 with mice, which (new at the time) provided a more intuitive way of interacting with a personal computer. We became the worldwide leader in computer mice, and have reinvented the mouse in dozens of ways to match the evolving needs of PC and laptop users.

      "Since those early days, we have expanded our expertise in product design beyond the computer mouse, with a broad portfolio of interface devices that are the 'last inch' between you and your computer or your console game, digital music or home-entertainment system.

      "With products sold in almost every country in the world, Logitech's leadership in innovation now encompasses a wide variety of personal peripherals (both cordless and corded), with special emphasis on products for PC navigation, gaming, Internet communications, digital music and home-entertainment control.

"For each of our product categories, we study how our customers use their digital devices, and then our designers and engineers set their sights on how we can create a better experience with those devices – richer, more comfortable, more fun, more productive, more convenient, more delightful."

- ○ Good: Asserts a unique position with its "personal peripherals" category, offers the value proposition that customers have a "better experience with the digital world," and uses the personalized verb *enjoy* to describe the experience.

- ○ Bad: Fails to emphasize leadership and fails to differentiate within the category. Also, too long.

- *Cree* strikes me as a Features Mechanic:

  - ○ Elevator story: "*Cree is a market-leading innovator of lighting-class LEDs, LED lighting, and semiconductor solutions for wireless and power applications.*"

  - ○ Good: Addresses role as market leader in the industry; statement is short and sweet.

  - ○ Bad: Fails to address "secret sauce" or uniqueness of solutions or technology; other than "leader," no differentiation.

Most of these positioning statements reveal the DNA of the company in their choice of language but fail to differentiate from there. The purpose of viewing the market through the lens of Competition is to enable you to define your company in a way that sets you apart from the competition, using DNA as a differentiation tool. It is designed to help you identify the white space in the market that only *you* can credibly fill. What is it about your DNA that enables you to capture a spot on the map and make it yours and yours alone? Who are you, and why do you matter?

What do these positioning statements need?

- As a Mechanic, Mobileye should call out its proprietary technology and approach.

- The Container Store must assert its Mother-knows-best customer service methodology.

- Verizon, which is transitioning from Mechanic to Mother, should explain "better" better.

- Logitech, another Mother, should address its unique user interface and how that results in a better customer experience.

- Mechanic Cree would do well to unpack "innovator" feature by feature.

Learn from the Best

Let's now examine a few great positioning statements, starting with Netflix (again, the positioning statements are italicized when they are embedded within the company's elevator story):

> "*Netflix is the world's leading Internet television network with over 93 million members in over 190 countries enjoying more than 125 million hours of TV shows and movies per day, including original series, documentaries and feature films.* Members can watch as much as they want, anytime, anywhere, on nearly any Internet-connected screen. Members can play, pause and resume watching, all without commercials or commitments."

This positioning statement pinpoints the company's role ("world's leading Internet television network") by calling out the leadership fact ("world's leading") and pointing to a relevant category that I believe Netflix coined ("Internet television network"). Notice, however, that it does not devote any space to catering to customers or focusing on their experience; nothing warm and fuzzy here. Nor, tellingly, does it highlight any value or features on offer.

Netflix is a Missionary with Next Big Thing written all over it, and it even alludes to having ignited what appears to be a movement (based on the vast footprint it has throughout the world). If you had spent the last few years living under a rock and didn't know what Netflix was, you'd learn from reading the positioning statement that Netflix leads in a new and relevant category, has tons of users already "enjoying" the service, and offers lots of original content.

What is Netflix? A leader in the Internet television network category. Why does it matter? Because a critical mass of people are using it (and you should, too).

Intuit is another good example, one that spans the B2C and B2B space:

"Intuit Inc. creates business and financial management solutions that simplify the business of life for small businesses, consumers and accounting professionals. Its flagship products and services include QuickBooks® and TurboTax®, which make it easier to manage small businesses and tax preparation and filing. Mint provides a fresh, easy and intelligent way for people to manage their money, while Intuit's ProConnect brand portfolio includes ProConnect Tax Online, ProSeries® and Lacerte®, the company's leading tax preparation offerings for professional accountants. Founded in 1983, Intuit had revenue of $4.7 billion in its fiscal year 2016. The company has approximately 7,900 employees with major offices in the United

States, Canada, the United Kingdom, India, Australia and
other locations."

Intuit's positioning statement all but shouts its DNA and genotype: a Mother with a focus on Segmentation. Here you see the role
of the company in what it does, for whom it does it, and why it matters to the customer: "[Intuit] creates business and financial management solutions that simplify the business of life for small businesses,
consumers and accounting professionals." The elevator story then
provides additional positioning statements for each of Intuit's significant products—and actually does double duty in terms of the overall corporate statement in that it reinforces the fact that the company
offers numerous tools for the management of small businesses.

Finally, let's look at a strong positioning statement from Zenefits,
a B2B company:

> *"Meet the #1 all-in-one HR platform for small business. Zenefits*
> *makes it easy to manage all your HR functions through a series of*
> *specialized apps. Each Zenefits app automatically shares its data*
> *with the other apps you use on the Zenefits platform, and all are*
> *easily accessed through a single online dashboard, eliminating*
> *thousands of hours in administrative work and enabling small*
> *businesses to run smoother."*

In short order, this Value Mechanic explains its role (an "all-in-
one HR platform"), its leadership position there ("#1"), and its target market ("small business"). It tells you what the product does and
describes the value to customers (Zenefits eliminates thousands of
hours in administrative work, enabling small businesses to run more
efficiently). And all without going soft and squishy like many of the
other HR platforms—most of which, of course, are Mothers. Zenefits
has differentiation right down to the DNA.

Your Turn

Now it's time for you to write your company's elevator story. But first, why do we call it an elevator story? Because it should be comprehensive enough to articulate what your company does and why it matters—all in the course of an elevator ride. Positioning is the core element of the elevator story, so write that first. Don't forget to check your Criteria list to make sure that what you wind up with is what you wanted to create. It should be a simple, fact-based, fluff-free declarative sentence that states your role and relevance in the market. Then combine all the pieces—Core, along with a smattering of Category, Community, Competition, and Context—into the unique mosaic that is your company for the elevator story.

If you get stuck, use the following "Mad Lib" as a tool to help you write your elevator story (but don't rely on it entirely): *"My Company, as an X (DNA type), is focused on X (genotype). We are an XX company (Category) providing XX (differentiated solution) to XX (target market). We (value proposition with a verb) by offering (some of the benefits of the product or service). Our product or service exists because (reason to exist at this time)."*

The first sentence is simply to get you centered on your DNA; it will not be part of the final positioning statement or elevator story. (In fact, although you won't ever reveal your Core DNA in words to your target audience, it will shine through in all your actions.) The second sentence is the core positioning statement and should reflect your DNA, as well as describe your role and relevance in the market. The third sentence offers your value proposition, and the final one answers the questions, "Why this product or service?" and "Why now?"

When you're done, reread the statement and ask yourself the following questions:

1. Does it reflect your DNA?

2. Does it pinpoint the white space you want to own and for whom?

3. Does it differentiate you from your competition?

4. Does it address why you matter?

5. Does it meet at least three-quarters of the criteria you set out for it?

If you can answer yes to each question, it's time to remove the grounding sentence about your DNA and genotype (because that's for you, not your market). You now have a positioning statement and an elevator story.

The Message Architecture

The next step is the message architecture, which provides the building blocks for your narrative. Message architecture is a framework of components that describe the company, with the positioning statement at the core. It also contains coherent branding elements and all the critical elements necessary for consistent and clear marketing and communication. In fact, it is the most important tool you'll have for communicating anything and everything. Also, you will find that it is an excellent tool for making business decisions, such as what kind of people to hire, how to build a culture, what M&A options to consider, how to measure success, and what markets to penetrate.

When it comes to message architecture, companies can learn a lot from politicians, who are well versed in what it means to be on message and off message. Being on message refers to using language that reflects the position of a certain candidate on a certain issue, whether it is specific or broad-based. Sound bites, phrases, and proof points are all supposed to reflect the position. Going off message means diverting from the original position. It also entails failing to reinforce a position with approved sound bites, phrases, and proof points. The more on message you are, the more opportunities you'll have to reinforce your place in the market. And the more you do it, the better. Good communication is about consistency and frequency, and your message architecture provides the foundation.

In fact, many studies show the importance of message frequency. The Marketing Rule of 7, for example, which was developed in Hollywood in the 1930s to help promote movies, holds that someone must hear a message at least seven times before being moved to take an action that could result in a purchase. Interestingly, hearing that message more than seven times seems to have a cumulative effect. It's safe to say, then, that you will become bored with your messaging long before a prospect has even begun to hear it. In light of the cacophony of messages we filter every day from social media, the Internet, television, radio, billboards, notifications, and conversations, however, it is likely that hearing something seven times is nowhere near enough to create resonance, let alone inspire a person to take an action.

But thanks to a plethora of channels from which to broadcast our messages, today, more than any time in history, we can take advantage of the human need to hear a message multiple times. We have owned channels—such as websites, blogs, newsletters, and social media—at our disposal. We have earned channels—our PR and analyst relations efforts—for which we create narratives to influence influencers. Finally, we have paid channels, which are composed of advertising and direct marketing in all its forms. All these channels can be used to exploit our messages and build a digital footprint (discussed in detail in Chapter 6) with the story we want to tell. But first we need messages that grow from the positioning statement.

Every opportunity to communicate, whether in web copy, a brochure, a sales meeting, a recruiting plea, a press release, a tweet, an ad, or even a conversation on an airplane, is another chance to repeat your message and, if all goes well, reach the Holy Grail of breaking through the noise. No opportunity should ever go unused!

The message architecture crystallizes your position in language and a voice that best captures the essence of your brand. I like to think of it as a messaging virus that is injected into any and all company communication vehicles. Just as a virus moves through a biological ecosystem, infecting and replicating as it goes, a message can infect a market ecosystem. This is why once you've done the work of creating the positioning statement and message architecture, you need to ensure that your message virus is disseminated frequently and consistently. Every time that message (or virus) is injected into a vehicle, it should look and sound exactly the same.

Although the DNA of such a virus generally remains consistent throughout its infectious journey, if something in the surrounding environment triggers a DNA change, the virus will change as well, and that particular infection won't occur. The same is true of messaging. Once that message architecture is complete, it shouldn't change as you disseminate it. The worst thing you can do is alter the frequency and consistency of your message once you put it out there. In fact, there are only two reasons to do that: if the market or environment has changed significantly enough to warrant tweaks or new messaging or if the messaging isn't resonating with the market. Never, however, change your message simply because you are bored with it.

What does all this mean? It means that your company must be described in exactly the same way every time and that the very same words must continue to be used throughout all forms of communication. Disseminated correctly, your message architecture will result in customers (and potential customers) absorbing your messages and beginning to attach your company's name and its products to the specific concepts you've outlined. You also should ensure that your branding elements are aligned with the positioning—that the look and feel, tone of voice, and personality are consistent with your role and relevance. And—if you are doing everything right—to the customer experience as well. Alignment in action! Authentic messages that align with a company's core identity have a better chance of sticking in the market than do those that don't. That's why we do the DNA positioning exercise.

A company's message architecture need not contain every element listed below, but it must contain the critical elements, which are target market, differentiator, category, value proposition, positioning statement, key messages, elevator story, brand archetype, brand personality, brand driver and narrative. This structure will give you the tools needed to inject the messaging virus into all of your external communication vehicles (including every owned, earned, and paid channel), as well as into your internal communication vehicles, including marketing (strategies, plans, campaigns), sales (training, sales enablement, pitch decks), and HR (onboarding, recruiting, engagement) (Figure 5.1).

Here is a compendium of all possible message architecture elements including vision, values, and related cultural mandates, the yin

Target market	The market you wish to serve with your product or service. These are your customers and your potential customers.
Differentiator	The single most palpable quality that makes you stand out from the competition.
Category	The group of peers in which your company belongs.
Value proposition	The key benefit you offer your most important customers. The primary reason a customer would buy from you.
Positioning statement	Articulates the differentiated role you play in your industry as well as your relevance to customers.
Key messages	The top three to five (no more!) messages that must be understood within a specific timeframe.
Elevator story	The corporate story in brief—just the facts.
Brand archetype	A genre you assign to your brand that is based on symbolism.
Brand personality	The personified traits that define your company.
Brand driver	The single word or phrase that best captures the essence of what your brand stands for.
Corporate narrative	The emotionally charged story of your company that answers the questions why your company? Why now?

FIGURE 5.1 Critical Elements of Message Architecture

of your identity (positioning) and the yang of your identity (branding). I illustrate each with elements from Cunningham Collective's (my consultancy) message architecture to help you write your own.

- **Vision:** The long-term mark you want to make on your customers, your industry, or the world at large; it should be relatively timeless and just out of reach. Think about how the world will be different because of your company.

  Cunningham Collective: Build brands that matter.

- **Values:** The core principles that guide the behavior of your employees. There are certain universal values that you may want to include, but the bulk of them should apply to your company, its DNA identity, and its value proposition. Shoot for five to seven.

  Cunningham Collective:

  o Embrace diverse perspectives.

  o Collaborate for high performance.

  o Think boldly.

  o Speak the truth.

  o Make an impact.

- **Our way:** The guidelines of behavior you'd like to instill in your employees to maintain a consistent face for the brand.

  Cunningham Collective:

  o Have the courage to say no.

  o Adopt a game-changing mentality.

  o Mentor someone.

  o Maintain personal integrity.

- Treat people fairly.

- Take intelligent risks.

- Be a team player.

- Keep others informed.

- Play an active role in the industry.

- Embrace new ideas and new technology.

- Stay current on management theories and industry events.

- See the forest as well as the trees.

- Contribute at every juncture.

- Find possibility where others don't.

- Strive for the highest quality.

- Help your clients win.

- Perform miracles.

- **Mission:** What you do every day in service to your vision. If employees can go home at night knowing they have done something specific to advance the company, they will be more engaged and better evangelists for the message.
  Cunningham Collective: Help our clients win.

- **Target market:** The market you wish to serve with your product or service. These are your customers and your potential customers.
  Cunningham Collective: Technology companies and companies that use technology to deliver products and services to their customers.

- **Target audience:** Your complete constituency: not only the target market but also the people who will influence your target market. It includes the press, analysts, bloggers, employees, users, consultants, and resellers, among others— anyone who might influence a customer.

  Cunningham Collective: Technology industry, including companies, analysts, press, venture capitalists, accelerators and incubators, and luminaries.

- **Differentiator:** The single most palpable quality that makes you stand out from the competition.

  Cunningham Collective: Strategic approach to communication based on business goals.

- **BHAG:** A Big Hairy Audacious Goal, as described by James Collins and Jerry Porras in their seminal book *Built to Last: Successful Habits of Visionary Companies.* A BHAG is an uber goal; it is visionary, strategic, and emotionally compelling.

  Cunningham Collective: Scale the firm to compete with McKinsey.

- **Category:** The group of peers in which your company belongs.

  Cunningham Collective: Branding, marketing, and communication agencies.

- **Value proposition:** The key benefit you offer your most important customers. It is not, however, everything you do, nor is it the most salient feature your product or service offers. It is the primary reason a customer would buy from you.

  Cunningham Collective: We help companies get traction in their markets.

- **Credo:** Many companies are founded on a strong belief that things can be different in the world because of them. This belief drives product development, employee management, and customer acquisition.

Cunningham Collective: We believe that great brands in the Digital Age are built on word of mouth and radiate from the intersection of strategic positioning and content marketing. We believe this is accomplished through the development of a compelling role and relevance clearly articulated within a persuasive narrative, one that is reinforced with a prodigious digital footprint.

- **Philosophy:** The ideology that drives your business; the underlying point of view you expect from your employees.

  Cunningham Collective: Our philosophy is rooted in the notion that image is based on substance and that positioning, the epicenter of image, is an articulation of what makes substance special. It is also a critical component of corporate competitiveness and the primary factor that leads to market success. This means positioning is at the core of everything we do. It also means we require the commitment and involvement of senior leadership throughout the process.

- **Positioning statement:** Articulates the differentiated role you play in your industry as well as your relevance to customers. This is the definitive statement of who you are and why you matter. Rooted in competitive advantage and differentiation, it is the unique statement that articulates your company within the white space you've defined.

  Cunningham Collective: Cunningham Collective is a Mother focused on Customer Experience. We are a brand strategy and execution firm providing a new and insightful way to position technology companies for traction in their markets.

- **What you do:** Large companies have a dual positioning challenge. They must articulate the role and relevance of the corporation and describe a variety of different products and services. During a turnaround, pivot, or relaunch (any of which could result in market confusion about your role), it is a good idea to have a statement that communicates what your company does at the highest level.

Cunningham Collective: We provide brand strategy based primarily on positioning and content marketing. We help companies get traction for their products and services by defining and articulating their unique position in the market and expressing that position through a number of executional initiatives and activities including content marketing.

- **What you offer:** It is useful to develop a description of your products and services that circles back to your corporate value proposition at the highest level. This statement (or statements) should answer the question, "What do you offer as a product or service?"

  Cunningham Collective:

  - Consulting services including brand, marketing, and communication strategy

  - Interim marketing and communication leadership

  - Execution services for brand building and rebuilding, market traction, and PR

  - Marketing-in-a-box including the complete marketing mix packaged for the particular needs of small companies

- **Strategic pillars:** How do you do what you do? Every company operates on a handful of pillars that represent the corporate strategy. They shouldn't be proprietary, but they should illuminate your highest-level strategy and may assist in differentiating your company.

Cunningham Collective:

○ Define a unique and effective framework.

○ Proliferate the methodology.

○ Do great work.

○ Create pull-through opportunities for execution.

○ Build a community of believers.

○ Scale the founder.

○ Partner strategically.

- **Key messages:** Beyond your positioning statement, there are always a handful of top-line key messages you wish to communicate to your most important audience. These are the top three to five (no more!) messages that must be understood within a specific time frame. They will evolve over time as the market shifts and the messages are absorbed. Developing a map of how you'd like these messages to change over time is a good way to time your messaging shifts and know when to make one. Your positioning should remain constant throughout.

  Cunningham Collective:

  ○ Corporate DNA matters.

  ○ Positioning and branding are yin and yang.

  ○ Success exists at the intersection of positioning and content marketing.

  ○ It is essential to master owned, earned, and paid channels of distribution.

  ○ Meticulous use of narrative builds a prodigious digital footprint.

- **Elevator story:** The corporate story in brief ("Just the facts, ma'am."). How would you describe your company in the length of time it takes to move between two floors in an elevator? It should contain the target market, the positioning statement, and one or two key elements from the message architecture.

  Cunningham Collective: Cunningham Collective is a Mother focused on Customer Experience. We are a marketing, brand strategy, and communication firm providing a new and insightful way to position technology companies for traction in their markets. We help our clients define their unique role and relevance with a proven strategic positioning framework that we take to market through mastery of owned, earned, and paid channels of content distribution, all with the objective of building a prodigious digital footprint.

- **Brand archetype:** A genre you assign to your brand that is based on symbolism. The idea is to anchor your brand to something iconic—something already embedded within what psychiatrist Carl Jung, the founder of the school of analytical psychology, called humanity's collective unconscious. We use an archetype system first developed by Jung in the mid-twentieth century and later adapted and tweaked by countless marketers. One of the exercises we do during the branding session entails handing out cards printed with the different archetypes, an activity that helps clients come to a conclusion about their company's brand. Once you know your company's archetype, you are better equipped to develop marketing initiatives that not only align with it but also enable better, more consistent, and more authentic communication. Pairing this emotional branding activity with the rational positioning exercise results in a complete picture of the yin and yang that is your brand. What follows are the 12 archetypes that, to

FIGURE 5.2 Brand Archetypes

varying degrees address four overarching themes: stability, independence, mastery, and belonging (Figure 5.2).

- **Ruler:** Leads people to a common destination through confidence, determination, and influence.

- **Creator:** Fashions something of enduring beauty and value.

- **Sage:** Finds the truth through research, objectivity, and diligence.

- **Explorer:** Seeks to change the environment.

- **Innocent:** Achieves a simple, pure life by always doing the right thing.

- **Maverick:** Attains freedom from the establishment through defiance and nonconformity.

- **Hero:** Protects others from harm through bravery and service.

- **Magician:** Helps others achieve experiences by promoting faith and wonder (often referred to as the Visionary).

- **Jester:** Relies on humor and fun to attract friends and avoid making enemies.

- **Everyman:** Bonds with others by being humble, hardworking, and friendly.

- **Lover:** Strives to be in a relationship with the surroundings.

- **Caregiver:** Helps others feel loved by providing for their needs and wants.

  Cunningham Collective: Primary Sage, Secondary Maverick.

- **Brand personality:** Just like humans, companies have character and personality traits that define them. Personality traits include friendly, feisty, bold, innovative, professional, conservative, peaceful, happy, and funny, among many others.

  Cunningham Collective:

  - Strategic

  - Smart

  - Stable

  - Clever

  - Enthusiastic

  - Thorough

  - Tactful

  - Honest

- ○ Dedicated

- ○ Just the right amount of geek

- **Brand driver:** The single word or phrase that best captures the essence of what your brand stands for. This is a word or phrase that describes your essence in nonemotional terms. It is not a tagline. Instead, it is a concept that informs all your touchpoints with customers.
  Cunningham Collective: Aha!

- **Brand attributes:** Brands, like people, have attributes that go hand in hand with personality traits. Attributes are not personified. Words such as *popular, entrenched, new, healthy, global,* and *local* are brand attributes.
  Cunningham Collective:

  - ○ Trusted

  - ○ Experienced

  - ○ High impact, low drama

  - ○ Efficient

  - ○ Understated

  - ○ Less is more

- **Brand promise:** The fundamental promise your brand makes to customers. The best brands offer a promise to return to customers an overarching benefit or value. Once the promise is made, it should never be broken.
  Cunningham Collective: Aha! with traction.

- **Ingredient brand:** Many brands muster power from being a key ingredient of something else. That ingredient transforms a standard product into one that is better, special, more interesting, healthier, faster, more vivid, and so forth. Ingredient brands (e.g., Intel Inside, NutraSweet, Dolby Surround) can power, enhance, and improve other products.

> *Cunningham Collective:* (Not applicable.)

- **Voice:** The choice of words and tone of voice you use to describe or illustrate your brand in words and visuals should align with your brand archetype and personality. Once you have this nailed, your copy and video will ring true.

  > *Cunningham Collective:*

  - Rational

  - Clear

  - Straightforward

  - Colloquial

  - Profound

  - Interesting

  - Insightful

- **Key phrases:** Every company develops a handful of phrases that help reinforce its position. Different from taglines (which are described below), they act as "color" in a narrative. Examples from the consumer world include "zero calories," "ideas worth spreading," "little green crystals," and "more smart, less phone."

  > *Cunningham Collective:*

  - Get to aha!

  - Innovation to market

  - Persuasive narrative

- ° Compelling role and relevance

- ° Who are you, and why do you matter?

- ° Corporate DNA

- ° The Six Cs of Positioning

- **Corporate narrative:** The emotionally charged story of your company. This is your chance to put your positioning into context. As always, the narrative should answer two questions: "Why your company?" and "Why now?" It should be persuasive, inspiring, convincing, and successful at converting prospects. You might want to publish the narrative in a "little brand book" or on the "About Us" section of your website.

  Cunningham Collective: In the early 1980s, our founder, Andy Cunningham, had the incredible opportunity to work with two of the tech industry's most visionary thinkers: Steve Jobs and Regis McKenna. It was during the momentous launch of the Macintosh that Andy discovered her craft. Working with Steve taught her to think boldly, make the impossible possible, and connect with customers emotionally. From Regis she learned that strategic positioning is the key to great marketing.

  Over the years, Andy honed these lessons into a philosophy and then a framework (and ultimately a book called *Get to Aha!*). That philosophy and framework led to the formation of Cunningham Collective, a marketing, brand strategy, and communication firm in the business of providing a new and insightful way to position companies for traction in their markets. Today's environment is noisier than ever due to the influx of communication channels enabled by the Internet. Getting your message heard is as hard as it has ever been. The tried and true approach of influencing the press to broadcast our corporate stories no longer works. Something had to change.

We apply Andy's proven strategic positioning framework to all our projects, helping clients define their unique role and relevance in the world. We then take their positions to market through mastery of owned, earned, and paid channels of content distribution with the objective of building a prodigious digital footprint. Through this process, we shape opinion and change behavior in the market to help our clients win.

We serve companies primarily in the technology sector and occasionally in other sectors that rely on technology to do what they do. Our expertise is understanding technology and positioning it for success. We define ideal positions, develop messages, and write narratives that enable companies to articulate their strategy and differentiation in a unique and compelling way. We then use various tactics to get their stories out and weave them into the market conversation.

To do this, we train and inspire internal teams on messaging; manage content development and distribution to define new stories; develop campaigns to create market awareness and generate interest; infiltrate marketing, sales, and HR communications; identify and educate influencers; place executives in the right place at the right time with the right messaging; and in some cases lead client communications teams and their agencies. We define or redefine technology brands by using language and various distribution channels to make it so. We promise aha! to our clients and that enables them to sell more products and services.

- **Tagline:** A brief and catchy phrase that sums up the primary value your company wants to express. If the positioning exercise is done correctly, taglines often emerge as if by magic. If this occurs, it is because of all the work that went into understanding the company's unique role and relevance as well as the emotional tug the tagline is meant to create. Taglines are frequently tied to the company's logo in a "lock-up" situation in which one does not appear without the other, thereby reinforcing the primary corporate value.

Cunningham Collective: Get to Aha!

To summarize, the message architecture contains all the tools you need to talk about your company at a high level with regard to marketing. Remember, marketing is about educating the market; it is about creating awareness of and interest in your company. As salespeople say, it "feeds the top of the funnel," meaning it prepares the target market for outreach from the sales team.

Note that the message architecture is a marketing document only and does not contain sales scripts, playbooks, or sales messages. Those are product/service/solution-focused and value-proposition-intense. As such, they must be constructed to address objections and competitive pitches. Certainly they should map to the larger corporate story, but by the time a salesperson is engaged with a potential customer, he or she probably will have been exposed to the higher-level messages in the message architecture and have some level of understanding of and appreciation for the company, product, or service. If this is not the case, the sales rep will have to start at the very beginning with the corporate story and then bridge into more specific product and market pitches.

This, of course, is why it is extremely useful to have the message architecture in a convenient and accessible place. We often create beautiful little books of a company's narrative for clients to give to employees and partners as a reminder of the corporate story. Elements of the message architecture should appear on the website and in advertising, PR, social media, HR materials, and everywhere else your company communicates.

6

Activation

You've done it. You know how you want to talk about your company. You know your precise place relative to the market's needs and opportunities, the competition, and the trends that are shaping your category. You know exactly how to articulate your role and relevance. You have a clear value proposition. Your key messages are compelling. Now it's time to tell the world.

But wait. How, exactly?

Companies are quick to celebrate when they get their ideal positioning down on paper. Too often, however, they fail to bring that positioning to life. The document outlining a marketing campaign may end up buried in a proverbial drawer. Or maybe it is beautifully projected by the CEO but not by the sales team. Or perhaps it results in a website refresh but fails to be embedded in the hearts and minds of prospects and customers. This chapter provides a framework for activating your positioning.

Bring Your Positioning to Life

Activating your positioning is what happens after your message architecture is in place. It is about bringing your company's message to life throughout the organization and out into the world. It's about thinking holistically and strategically about how to connect activities, touchpoints, communication vehicles, events, and even the physical environment with key messages. Activating positioning does not mean just adjusting your marketing communication; it's not simply a matter of the marketing department going off and rewriting some copy or updating the website. It doesn't mean just changing the boilerplate on your press releases or creating a new PowerPoint slide or a novel visual identity. Instead, activating positioning requires the injection of your positioning and key messages into *all* your communication vehicles and ensuring that your internal and external audiences receive precise and frequent doses. Activating your positioning means preparing your team members to understand how their roles connect to this new articulation of your strategy and what they have to do to support it.

Before we launch into specifics, here is the secret to activating any new positioning: treat it as you would treat a product launch. Like any well-executed, holistically designed launch, your new positioning launch should do all of the following and nothing less:

- Prepare your company to market and support the new positioning.

- Prime the market to understand and embrace the new positioning and then reach that market.

- Protect your existing customers and your relationships with them.

Positioning Activation

The high-priority targets for your new positioning rollout are probably obvious: your website, your sales materials, maybe a sign in your lobby or the wording on your packaging. But you'll need to think more holistically to bring your positioning to life. Deploying a new position requires the consideration of both internal and external audiences, the points at which they intersect, and the channels of distribution used to reach them. Internal factors consist of company alignment and culture, sales enablement, delivery, and support. You must master your *owned* and *paid* channels of distribution. External factors encompass a company's public face, its marketing and PR, and customer reactions. You must master your *earned* channels of distribution (Figure 6.1).

As you go about activation, don't forget to think of positioning and branding as yin and yang, two interconnected but distinct sides of your company's identity.

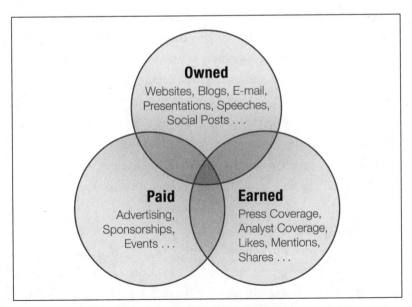

FIGURE 6.1 Message Channels

You'll recall that positioning is the yin; it represents the rational expression of your strategy. It articulates your role and relevance in your market. Branding is the yang; it is the emotional expression of your strategy and consists of the "softer side" of your brand, including personality, brand attributes, look and feel, and tone of voice. Other yang elements include the company's logo and tagline, environment, and materials—everything from the lobby to the website and business cards. The yin and the yang come together in the message architecture, which outlines your target market, differentiator, category, value proposition, positioning statement, key messages, elevator story, brand archetype, brand personality, brand driver, and corporate narrative, among other things.

Getting Everyone on the Same Page

As always, the connective tissue between the internal and the external is alignment: strategy and positioning alignment within the C-suite and message alignment throughout the company and out into the market. It is this alignment, along with consistency and frequency of message, that offers the greatest advantages to growth because it forces all the parts of the company to row in one direction all the time.

Certainly leadership plays a critical role in all this, but it is positioning that provides the compass for the decisions made in every department. The advantages of doing a rigorous positioning exercise are many, and the payoff can be exponential. Here are five obvious benefits:

- **Energy efficiency:** When all the parts of the company are focused on a single point on the compass where role and relevance are paramount, the entire entity can move in that direction. The result? You get there faster using less energy. So many companies spin their wheels deploying time and money in multiple directions when a clear position and brand could provide all the guidance needed to avoid that.

Cisco is an example of a company in which energy efficiency was done right. Shortly after he became CEO, John Chambers reached out to me to discuss how we might be able to help him elevate the company above the day-to-day business of selling hubs and routers and achieve his goal of engaging all employees in a concerted effort to increase the corporate valuation.

This was the mid-1990s, and we correctly surmised that the emerging Internet would change the face of communications forever. Cisco, at its core, was a communications company that provided the plumbing that made the Internet hum. So, we thought, why not create a position in the market that not only gives Cisco credit for the Internet, but also make it compelling enough that employees will aspire to something greater? (Not to mention equally compelling to the market in the hopes of achieving a higher valuation.)

We put together a thought leadership platform we called "Cisco and the Internet Economy." At that time, there were only two CEOs who dominated the technology airwaves: Intel's Andy Grove represented the hardware side, and Microsoft's Bill Gates the software end. No one then had any inkling that the inclusion of the Internet would offer the third leg that would turn that duopoly into a triad. Well, no one but us! We gambled that we would be able to add it as a critical vector and position John Chambers as the leader who would make it happen. To that end, we commissioned the University of Texas to conduct a study quantifying the opportunity the Internet represented. We dubbed it "The Internet Economy Study," published it widely through our own channels, and used it as the foundation of a PR campaign, both to educate the market and to introduce Cisco—and specifically John Chambers—as the owner of the narrative we'd created. We also uploaded self-assessments to Cisco's website that other companies could use on their path to becoming Internet-ready, overhauled John's calendar to ensure that he limited his speaking engagements to events at which only Andy Grove and Bill Gates were speaking, and ensured that his speeches focused on the high-level topic of the Internet economy and what it meant for humanity.

The press quickly adopted "the Internet Economy" as a phrase and subsequently coined "WinTelCo" as a moniker to refer to all three companies. The result was a home run. Cisco was forever connected to the Internet, John's cachet sky-rocketed as he joined the tech industry's pantheon of most important CEOs, the company's valuation climbed from $1.2 billion in 1995 when John became CEO to $43 billion in 1997, and employees banded together to create products that ultimately would make the Internet economy reliant on Cisco. It goes to show you that a great product, a visionary CEO, and a compelling narrative can come together to build a world-class brand.

- **Resource preservation:** People and investment resources are a company's most important assets. Deploying those resources for growth should be job number one. Providing direction for that deployment seems simple enough, but in a company with numerous people and departments, it isn't as straightforward as it sounds. Even small companies have issues with this. You have a financial goal, you have deadlines for development, you have someone doing something in marketing, and you've got salespeople on the phone. At first glance, how hard can it be? In fact, it can be very difficult if, at the highest level, people don't have a vision and mission to point them in the right direction and they struggle to answer these two questions: "Who are we?" and "Why do we matter?" Positioning provides the alignment to make answering these questions possible.

Twitter is a great example of a company that has lost resource after resource in an ongoing journey to "find itself." According to a *New Yorker* article from January 29, 2016, the company had experienced a "massive executive brain drain" the previous summer. The author noted, "What should worry Twitter is irrelevance, and there is growing data to suggest that is where the company is headed." Relevance, of course, is a matter of positioning.

- **Focused attention:** Success is most likely when a group (a software company, a sports team, a pack of wolves) is focused on a particular outcome. Each individual may have a specific job, but they all have a common focus. If the company, team, or pack is working as it should, every member knows what the group is trying to accomplish and is aligned with that accomplishment. The result? The software company launches a successful product, the team wins, the wolves eat. But if focus is lacking, disaster ensues.

  As an example, look no further than Yahoo!, a company with 1 billion users and thus seemingly endless opportunity. Even so, it's clear the company hasn't been able to pinpoint its role and relevance no matter how many iterations of leadership it experiences. No doubt this is the reason for countless reorganizations, the most recent being the Verizon acquisition leading to the mashup with AOL now called Oath. Since it is known as an advertising, content, search, and mobile platform, you'd think Oath (formerly Yahoo!) would be able to com-

pete successfully with Google and Facebook, the two dominant online advertising firms in the country. And in fact, that
seems an obvious strategy now that Verizon has acquired the
company and has made no secret of its desire to move into
third place behind those giants. Still, a strategy to compete
head on with the other two giants is not a positioning statement. Google is an ad platform that is based on search, one
that is ingrained in the daily habits of millions. Facebook is
also an ad platform, but it is based on a social network made
up of family and friends. What is Oath? What value does it
provide? Without an answer to these questions, Verizon probably will find itself struggling with the same identity issues
that plagued Carol Bartz and Marissa Mayer when they were
successive CEOs of Yahoo!.

- **Buy-in and adoption:** Getting your rowers synchronized
  entails involving them in the positioning process. No matter
  how solid a position is, without buy-in no one will adopt
  it. And positioning is worthless unless people use it—yet
  another reason every member of the C-suite must be involved
  in the positioning process (and beyond). I've had people
  ask, "Why in the world do you need the CFO involved with
  marketing?" Because of buy-in. We always include CFOs
  (and every other C-suiter) in the positioning exercise because
  when it's time for the CFO to start executing on the financial
  side of the equation, he or she must not only understand
  the desired outcome, but also be committed to it. And
  commitment is much more likely from someone who was
  involved in formulating the plan, whose fingerprints are all
  over it. The only way to assure C-suite (and thus companywide) buy-in and adoption is by including everyone in the
  process. Consistency is key. After all, positioning is a team
  sport! Or at least it should be.

A case in point: During Hector Ruiz's leadership of the
Motorola Semiconductor Products Sector in the late 1990s,
he invited me to be a part of his "semiconductor redefinition
group."The international working group was led by a facilita-
tor who was charged with reorganizing the sector and focusing it on opportunities for the future, and Ruiz launched the
yearlong process by announcing the Hector Ruiz Principle
described in Chapter 3: 60 percent agreement, 100 percent
buy-in. This rule of engagement enabled a disparate group of
executives from all over the world to, in short order, introduce
ideas, coalesce around the good ones, and decide on direction. Over the years, I have used this rule repeatedly, and I
deploy it in positioning exercises whenever I need to break a
stalemate. It eliminates groupthink, indecision, and too much
consensus building.

- **Coalescence:** I often tell new clients that I already know
  their positioning statement without having to talk to them.
  It's obvious: they want to be all things to all people. That
  always gets a laugh, because, of course, a product or service
  can never be all things to all people. It can, however, be
  something to someone, and the sooner the C-suite coalesces
  around that something and embraces it, the stronger the
  company's sense of motivation and overall alignment will
  be. Every person brings a different skill set to the table,
  and just as with a sports team, the success or failure of any
  venture is in great part dependent on how well those leaders
  work together and how connected they are to one another—
  that is, whether they work in synergy and coalesce around
  whatever their North Star is.
  As was mentioned in Chapter 4, we worked with
  BlackBerry to change the narrative from one limited to hardware to a compelling new one focused on software. Because

BlackBerry is no longer the unrivaled leader in smartphones that it was several years ago and because under the guidance of turnaround CEO John Chen the company is pivoting to enterprise security software, we decided that our BHAG was to "reposition the company for a new relevance." During the positioning process we uncovered the Enterprise of Things (EoT) white space and subsequently decided on the following positioning statement: "BlackBerry is a mobile-native security software and services company dedicated to securing the Enterprise of Things."

The positioning exercise involved the entire leadership team, of course, and everyone contributed to the discussion. After a bit of skepticism about the Enterprise of Things white space—then an unfamiliar term to the team—everyone came to embrace the opportunity, and John made it clear that the company was headed in the direction of owning EoT security. The payoff? After we developed the full narrative—which appears later in this chapter and was written to inspire employees to engage in the new BlackBerry—it soon became clear that every division of the company was telling the story in meetings and via blog posts and social media. It has even shown up in HR recruiting materials. To reinforce this coalescence narrative (particularly for future hires), we created a "little brand book." By this point it has become the BlackBerry story—the one with which everyone connects. And we got there because a key group of leaders in the company participated in the work and bought into the outcome.

When your team coalesces around the yin and the yang of your brand, you are rewarded with evangelism. Everyone begins to sing from the same hymn book—in harmony—until it becomes a choir.

From Message Architecture
to Market Resonance

Okay, you've got executive buy-in. The message architecture is built. The narrative is compelling. It is time to infect first the company and then the market with the positioning virus. The goal here is to move from message architecture to market resonance.

Regardless of how many employees work at your company, each and every one of them should be an evangelist for your story. So first things first: train them.

I find that this training is best done in small groups—in person, if possible, and with a small set of slides that reinforces the message. The best person to do the training is someone who is senior, credible, and a good communicator. The key here is to use these sessions as opportunities to inspire the workforce to carry the message forward. I usually start the sessions by asking the group members if they've ever found themselves on an airplane having to answer such questions as "Where do you work?" and "What does your company do?" We've all been there, and many of us, especially in technology, end up spitting out a whole lot of words that don't seem to mean anything. I tell them that the new company narrative will change all that and that they have a role to play in evangelizing the new narrative. The company needs their help.

I then read them the narrative that we created. I know that reading is anathema to a seasoned presenter, but for this particular purpose I find it to be effective. It's the company's new story, and using the proper tone of voice and word inflection is critical to its communication. As is the presentation itself, which is why in addition to illustrating the narrative through slides, I face the audience and work hard to be animated.

Here is the narrative we created for BlackBerry, which is also the script I read to each and every department of the company:

Once upon a time, BlackBerry was a giant in the land of smartphones. Most people who needed or wanted one had a BlackBerry. We invented much of what the smartphone is today, and we built one of the world's most globally recognized brands. We were the market leaders, and we ruled the roost. But more than that, we developed a strong emotional connection with our customers that persists even today. They love us.

But the market changed. Apple introduced the iPhone. Google brought Android to market. Suddenly, competition was everywhere and moving fast. We weren't fast enough. We lost our grip and fell behind. We watched our market share drop significantly and our relevance diminish over time. But all the while we continued to innovate in connected security and mobility, and we began to focus that innovation on software rather than hardware.

That's when our board brought in a new CEO. John Chen joined us as our leader in 2013 after a very successful stint turning around Sybase. He recognized our legacy and believed that BlackBerry could be a leader again, but this time by taking advantage of our software, security, and mobility assets and phasing out the manufacture, distribution, and marketing of handsets. And we are nearly there. In addition to our new leadership and the focus on software, we are also blessed with the market conditions to win. The time is right for BlackBerry to be a leader again.

Network connectivity among objects, devices, and computers promises to transform the way we live, work, and play. The Internet of Things is emerging as one of the most significant developments of our time. Connecting people and things will be the new norm for consumers, but behind the scenes, it is transforming how enterprises develop, market, distribute, and sell products. The "Enterprise of Things" is upon us.

These expanding connections are exponentially accelerating our vulnerability. Data breaches and cybersecurity threats are some of the biggest roadblocks to realizing the greatest potential of the Enterprise of Things. Businesses must be able to confidentially and reliably transmit sensitive data between endpoints to keep people, information, and goods safe.

Market demand for security is shifting from the network of computers to the network of endpoints, and traditional security software players are scrambling to fill this gap. BlackBerry is uniquely qualified to address this emerging market need now because of the company's legacy leadership and ongoing innovation in securing and managing mobile devices. BlackBerry is no longer about the smartphone, but the smart in the phone—and in cars and containers, medical devices and wearables, consumer appliances and industrial machinery, and ultimately the entire enterprise. BlackBerry software provides the embedded intelligence to secure the Enterprise of Things so that the Internet of Things can thrive.

We intend to be a leading software company with a standard of security that manages the network of endpoints within the enterprise. In addition to developing and acquiring our applications, we are enabling customers to develop their own applications, and building a community of developers to create third-party applications.

BlackBerry, and its associated applications, are showing up in every industry where secure mobile communications are critical. For example, our software:

- Prevents hackers from penetrating devices and computers

- Provides intelligence for secure supply chain communications

- Ensures patient confidentiality in healthcare

- Enables secure communications throughout product development and distribution cycles

- Allows construction projects to safely run on schedule connecting mobile devices with corporate project management

- Offers highly secure mobile communications for thousands of geographically disperse consultants and their clients

- Safeguards assets in the financial industry

- Manages crisis communications between and among government agencies and forces

- Affords secure and seamless communications for global employee networks in consumer goods and retail

- Protects proprietary data from competitive assault

Swag and Such

The next part of the training session consists of going through and explaining the different elements of the message architecture so that the audience can understand what each one is, why it was written that way, and how it ultimately fits into the overall narrative. Finally, it is critical to outline everyone's role in telling the story—and to give each person the tools to do so. I find that a small and portable "brand book" works well for this. Not only is it the story of the company, it is also *their* story (Figure 6.2).

FIGURE 6.2 Brand Books

It may sound silly, but swag (stuff we all get) helps a lot. People like free stuff. T-shirts are always a big hit with tech companies (though make sure they are high quality; you want people to wear them). But hats, mugs, screen savers, wristbands, and drink bottles are great as well. Pick a portion of the story to reprint on the various items of swag and you've got a permanent reminder of the new narrative. And if the dissemination is done with some flare—say, accompanied by a funny video—you can show employees that the new narrative is cool. The goal is to get everyone talking about it—and using it—exactly the way it was written.

In addition to training employees, you've got to make sure that the various departments throughout the company are not only using the narrative but also making departmental decisions with the new narrative in mind. This is especially critical for marketing and communications; all communications must be infused with the narrative. And don't forget about HR. Every bit of recruiting and onboarding collateral must reflect the new narrative. You want to attract potential hires with your message and immediately make evangelists out of new employees. The senior leadership team should be conversing in your narrative at all meetings and creating strategies and plans that take it into consideration. It's everyone's job to make the narrative the language of choice for your company.

Finally, don't forget about the sales team. These are the people who are closest to the customer, and so their ability to tell the new story is critical. They should have the story down pat and be able to connect it to the individual products and services they sell. Connective tissue must be built to bridge the corporate vision articulated in the narrative and specific product points. Because the team will need help with this, make sure you build a cohesive story for each product and each vertical market. Each story, in turn, should be translated into sales enablement tools and made easily accessible.

Next up is taking the narrative to market. How do you get the outside world to take notice? It's all in the mastery of your channels of message distribution. Marketing has responsibility for owned, earned, and paid channels of message dissemination, and every scrap of language must contain the virus. That means the website, the blog, social media, brochures, sales enablement materials, press releases, advertisements, direct marketing and e-mail campaigns, speeches, white papers, trade show booths, and signage. Everything.

The tools are critical here. You'll need to get your marketing team to create blocks of content that are based on the narrative that can be infused easily into each and every one of these channels. You'll need blocks for every conceivable application. Some will be 140-character tweets; others will be longer blocks that are white-paper-worthy. You'll need phrases and paragraphs, and you'll need signs and slogans. In short, you'll need a library of content that has been injected with the virus.

The goal of all these blocks, of course, is activation. The objective is to build as large a digital footprint as your budget will allow by using content marketing tactics. Small companies with small budgets will have to rely primarily on owned channels. That's okay. Thanks to the Internet, we have dozens of these: websites, blogs, YouTube, Instagram, Twitter, Snapchat, Facebook, LinkedIn, Medium, podcasts, speeches, customer communications, and newsletters. You also should include earned channels: public relations, analyst relations, and investor relations. Make sure every press release and advisory, not to mention pitch, meeting, and press conference, contains the language. Infuse it into all analyst briefings. Get the messaging into the earnings calls. Put it everywhere and get everyone saying the same thing. In addition, if you have the budget for agency support, ensure that everything they create has the virus.

Last but not least, master your paid channels. All direct, field, and partner marketing should contain the narrative. Make sure any advertising of any kind includes the messaging too. The bigger your budget is, the more you'll be able to blanket the market with your story.

It should take about three months to infect all channels and build your digital footprint. And of course, the bigger the digital footprint, the better. Using one of the many analytics tools available for measuring market resonance—such as brand surveys, media monitoring, social tracking, sentiment analysis, and share of voice—you should be able to tell if the story is sticking. In my experience, a sticky message is a bit like pornography. It's difficult to measure, but you know it when you see it. In fact, a sticky story should be palpable. You should start to see changes in press coverage, customer response, employee engagement, and the like. All of these can be analyzed to death, but you'll know it if and when it's happening. And if it isn't, you'll know that something is wrong or has changed, and you'll move quickly to tweak the messaging. If you've done your positioning right, if you've selected a white space that no one owns, and if you've taken into consideration the six Cs of positioning discussed in Chapter 4—especially Context—you should be able to achieve traction within one quarter. The bigger the budget, the quicker the traction, of course, but all this can be done on the cheap by blanketing your owned channels with a compelling message.

As everyone is brought within the new narrative, the alignment and positioning virus spreads throughout the organization. The result is less friction and fewer factions. Remember Ken Olsen's hundred thousand canoes, each paddling in a different direction? Alignment takes care of that, leaving you with a streamlined vessel that can surge forward with maximum power.

7

Genetic Engineering

What if there is tension between who you are as a company and how you think you want to position? Is it possible to change your DNA?

Yes, you *can* change your company's DNA, but it's not easy. And it's not a decision to be taken lightly.

Most companies continue for years, decades, even generations in DNA rubber-stamp mode. And why wouldn't they? Mother, Mechanic, or Missionary behavior is baked into their genetic code. Oracle, for example, appears to be happily, solidly a Mechanic. It's not looking to shoot rockets into space or even to design a next-generation driverless car. Rather than branching out into new territory, it seems perfectly content to continue developing and marketing integrated cloud applications and platform services for the foreseeable (and presumably lucrative) future, upgrading and supplementing existing features as it goes. Also, any company it considers adding to its arsenal probably will be a fellow Mechanic, as has been the case over the years when it has acquired Sun Microsystems, Taleo, Eloqua, Responsys, and NetSuite.

Similarly, companies such as Nike, the *Wall Street Journal*, Nordstrom, Etsy, and Disney come across as devoted to motherhood; they have always catered to their customers' needs and wants and show no signs of changing their focus. A Mother is what they are, what they've always been, and all indications suggest, what they wish to remain. As Stefan Thomke and Donald Reinertsen note in their article "Six Myths of Product Development," which appeared in the *Harvard Business Review*, "When Walt Disney was planning Disneyland, he didn't rush to add more features (rides, kinds of food, amount of parking) than other amusement parks had. Rather, he began by asking a much larger question: How could Disneyland provide visitors with a magical customer experience?"

What, however, would it mean if Disney suddenly began focusing on rides, food, and parking at the expense of customer experience? Such a shift in attention would indicate a DNA shift from Mother to Mechanic.

Genetic Design

Although DNA changes are uncommon, a company can, in fact, make a choice to alter its genetic makeup. Amazon, for example, started out as a Missionary, and remnants of that DNA remain. A genetic change, however, is currently under way. As was noted in an article in the *New York Times* about Amazon dropping list prices from the site, the company "is in the middle of an ambitious multiyear shift from a store selling one product at a time to a full-fledged ecosystem." It also has expanded its retailing platform to build a multibillion-dollar stream of web services. Over the years the company has morphed into a Mother, dedicated to ensuring that customers get exactly what they want, and quickly. To that end, Amazon probably has initiated specific companywide strategy shifts in the way it hires, trains, and compensates its employees; the way it is structured; the way it measures success; and so on—all in true Mother form, with a goal of radically improving an already existing service. One of the biggest indicators of that shift, of course, was Amazon's 2009 purchase of Zappos, a company renowned for excellent customer service. Rather than overhaul Amazon from the inside out, CEO Jeff Bezos appears to have determined that the best and easiest way to achieve a customer-first mindset was to acquire a company that wrote the book on it (or at least *a* book, in the form of Zappos CEO Tony Hsieh's *Delivering Happiness*, which describes how to create a positive, customer-focused company culture). As a result, Hsieh told the *Wall Street Journal*, Amazon has implemented certain Zappos practices throughout the larger organization, including paying new employees in select departments to quit after a few weeks if they find the company is a poor fit.

For a snapshot of the way Amazon's focus and DNA have changed over the years, consider that when it first launched its online presence in 1995, the primary thing the company wanted us to know about it was that it was "Earth's biggest bookstore." Amazon's official statement today is quite different and far more aspirational: "Our vision is to be Earth's most customer centric company; to build a place where people can come to find and discover anything they might want to buy online." And so they can, with glow-in-the-dark toilet paper, engagement rings, and uranium ore only a click away. As Bezos famously said in an interview, "What's dangerous is not to evolve."

Google, now Alphabet, is another company that has driven a DNA change, in this case from Mechanic to Missionary. Although it once was dedicated exclusively to all things search, the company has expanded its focus over the years to the Next Big Thing(s)—everything from biotech to artificial intelligence, from renewable energy to self-driving cars. There is no question that its DNA switch was purposeful. In a 2014 interview with the *Financial Times*, Google cofounder Larry Page declared that the company was "looking to take on more things of significant impact to people" and that it would be "amazing if we can do that at a bigger scale than we're doing." In fact, he admitted that the company had outgrown its original mission statement: "Google's mission is to organize the world's information and make it universally accessible and useful." In light of the company's evolution, Page said, the big question was, "How do we use all these resources we have and have a much more positive impact on the world?" This is clearly a moonshot mentality and one that prompted the company to stretch well beyond its earliest ambitions—to "think different," as Steve Jobs would say.

It'll Cost You

Of course, another aspect of the Google transition from Mechanic to Missionary is that, as a result of its search and web advertising dominance, Alphabet is now a company with a staggering amount of cash on hand to pour into whatever research and development it fancies. Having so many resources at its disposal means it can give really, really smart people millions of dollars simply to play around with interesting ideas for as long as it takes for them to come up with a promising notion (or not). When a germ of an idea takes hold, the company's overflowing coffers once again ensure that there is plenty of money to support that idea all the way from concept to production. "We do benefit from the fact that once we say we're going to do it, people believe we can do it, because we have the resources," Page told the *Financial Times.* "Google helps in that way: there aren't many funding mechanisms like that." Indeed, as the *Guardian* noted, "Page's attitude is 'well, somebody's got to do it' and Google's resources allow it to do more than most."

That leads to my next point where genetic engineering is concerned. Beyond basic logistics, there's something else to consider if you're thinking about a DNA change: in addition to time and effort, it takes a significant sum of money to restructure a company. No one remakes a company, particularly an established company, by fiat alone. It's not a decision that a CEO sleeps on overnight and then announces the next day. A lot goes into a DNA overhaul of any kind.

Say you're a Mechanic with a quarter-century track record and you want to become a Mother, to shift from product orientation to customer satisfaction. It sounds great in theory, but there are a thousand different hurdles standing in your way, beginning with the fact that a company doesn't survive that long without developing a few entrenched habits and procedures. For example, many old-school Mechanics, particularly the bigger ones, don't always know who their customers are. Why? Because they've spent the last 10 years, maybe the last 30 years, selling their products through distribution channels. That means that it's the distribution-channel people who best know the customers' likes and dislikes, their needs and wants, not the Mechanic itself. But since a Mother must know her customers inside and out, the company will need to work overtime to wrestle those relationships back into the fold, most likely by first changing its sales structure from a distribution model to a direct one. That's a transition that takes time, know-how, and a lot of money. It's not just a matter of saying, "Okay, everybody. We're going to go left now instead of right." You'll need to overhaul your sales force. You'll need to hire different people, train them differently, and compensate them differently. From here on out, you'll even measure success according to a new standard. Everything has to be reconsidered and revamped, and all from the ground up.

Once you expand this scenario across every department in the company, you can begin to appreciate how daunting and expensive a challenge you're facing. For most companies, an operation of this magnitude is overwhelming, and the patient probably will die on the table.

Simply put, changing DNA requires rewiring a company in nearly every way. To continue the example of a Mechanic looking to make a genetic switch, keep in mind that successful rewiring of a product-oriented company almost always entails killing off a product or two and perhaps even more, an action that more often than not is antithetical to the Mechanic mindset (although to its credit, even in its staunchest Mechanic days, Google never appeared to be overly shy about retiring products, popular or otherwise). In general, probably the worst thing you can propose to a group of engineers is that they pull the plug on one of their babies. Engineers at every level, including (and maybe especially) the product manager as well as those populating the C-suite, have been known to do almost anything to keep pet creations alive. The engineering organism that is at the heart of the company simply refuses to shut them down, and troubled but beloved—to the company, if not the customer—products are routinely put on life support when they should be euthanized.

It's a problem that's been around for as long as there have been engineers. For example, someone at General Motors was clearly infatuated with the Iron Duke, a four-cylinder engine the company stuffed under the hood of way too many car models from the late 1970s to the early 1990s. As engines go, it was rough, coarse, and widely derided, but one business manager or another over the years refused to let it die. A more recent example of a product that outlasted its welcome is Microsoft's Outlook for Windows, which grew increasingly stale and irritating over the years thanks to endless bugs and crashes. The same could be said of Microsoft's Internet Explorer. In both cases, it's likely that a substantial number of users put up with the situation only because the programs were embedded in their employers' systems.

Food for Thought

Nonetheless, even though companywide restructuring to facilitate a DNA change requires substantial time and money, if you're really determined to overhaul your genetics, rest assured that you don't have to be an Alphabet—or even an Amazon—backed by hundreds of billions in assets to do it. Nor are you required to have the aspirations that often go with that amount of money. Wolfgang Puck, for example, isn't out to change the world; he simply wants to change the way it eats. Originally a passionate chef and restaurateur devoted primarily to gratifying customers' palates individually (a textbook definition of a Mother if there ever was one), Puck over the last 30-plus years has built a culinary empire composed of restaurants, high-end kitchenware, and commercial foods. In short, he has become a Mechanic, dedicated to his product first and foremost. As he wrote in a "How I Did It" essay for *Inc.*, "Success for me has always been focusing on the product first, the money second, whether that is a can of soup, a frying pan, or a restaurant." He may see himself as "focusing on the product first," but in truth, as a young chef, he focused on building a community of loyal customers, which was necessary to do before building a line of products that had market credibility and could sell themselves from an airport stand.

Regardless of the reason behind a DNA change, the transition is always easier when it is initiated by a leader with a strong personality that is big enough to inspire people to move from one deeply entrenched—and most likely comfortable—place to another. This is why it helps to have a Cult of Personality leader at the helm during a purposeful DNA change. It's even better if that Cult of Personality leader is also the company founder, able to imbue the switch with additional urgency. In fact, being a Cult of Personality leader *and* founder all but gives you a license to kill, so to speak. Employees who followed a leader before will be more likely to follow that leader again even when the transitioning ground beneath them grows increasingly shaky.

Genetic Mutation

Thus far we've focused on companies that *choose* to alter their genetic code. Sometimes, however, DNA changes by itself as a result of the environment surrounding the company undergoing a change. There's an episode of *Star Trek: The Next Generation* titled "Genesis" that I like to use as an analogy. A virus on the ship causes crew members and other living creatures to devolve into more primitive lifeforms: reptile, amphibian, monkey, prehistoric human, and the like. Something in the environment triggers the DNA changes. In addition to the physical metamorphoses, the genetic revisions cause altered behavior. All the changes are incremental at first—on her way to transforming into an amphibian, Deanna Troi, the ship's counselor, finds herself perpetually cold and is compelled to take hot baths; as he reverts to a slow-witted caveman, First Officer Will Riker gradually loses his ability to concentrate—but as cells continue to mutate, changes that once were brushed off as random and insignificant become overt and overwhelming.

The same thing happens with companies undergoing a genetic shift. Just as Troi's curious but seemingly harmless desire to spend all her time in the bathtub even when fully clothed was indicative of the alterations taking place on a genetic level, companies often are unaware of DNA changes that are under way until they become more obviously apparent, as in the hypothetical (and highly unlikely) case of Disney turning its focus to rides, food, and parking at the expense of customer experience. Once those changes do become apparent, however, it is up to the leadership team to decide whether to allow the transformation to continue—indeed, to work proactively on a strategic level to encourage it—or to find a way, as on *Star Trek*, to shut it down and reverse the effects.

Many inadvertent, sneak-up-from-behind company DNA changes result from maturation. (Corporate DNA shifts generally signal some form of evolution, not devolution, as in the *Star Trek* scenario.) Most companies, if they ever see a genetic change at all, will see it happen only once, maybe twice, in a 25-year lifetime as a business moves from the start-up stage to firmer ground, for example, or as a company matures after many years as an established entity. Whatever the time frame, something in the environment changes, and that alteration automatically triggers a gradual shift in behavior. The company will begin to measure success slightly differently. It will begin to hire different people. It will begin to train those new employees to different standards. In such cases, the changes are gradual, almost surreptitious, as on *Star Trek*, where the characters' DNA mutations are, initially at least, so subtle as to go unnoticed. Something in the environment changes, and that change causes an evolution in functioning.

IBM is a great example of a company that has undergone many shifts over the course of its more than 100-year existence, each time rising from the apparent ashes of its former self to new heights. Not surprisingly, a few of those makeovers over the last century have involved DNA shifts. For example, when Sam Palmisano took over the reins from Lou Gerstner in 2002, he set about remaking the company once again—even after Gerstner had done a pretty good job remaking it during his reign (about which he wrote a seminal book called *Who Says Elephants Can't Dance?*). Palmisano's pivot, however, involved a DNA change from Mechanic to Mother, which was prompted by a desire to take advantage of an industrywide movement from hardware to services and software. As it turns out, the CEO's makeover was a smart one that stemmed from the realization that the company had outgrown its once-treasured sweet spot: "The corporate technology industry is scrambling for higher ground, moving from hardware into services and mixing in some business software," Steve Lohr of the *New York Times* wrote in a 2010 article. "The goal is steady revenue, higher profits and tighter bonds with customers—and the model is I.B.M.," which Lohr noted had enjoyed a record year of profits.

In that environment, Palmisano realized that the product mix had to change—and with it, the DNA of the company. "Since Samuel J. Palmisano became chief executive in 2002," Lohr continued, "I.B.M. has spent more than $25 billion on dozens of acquisitions, nearly all services and software companies. The company's big research arm has been retooled to tilt toward services, and it worked with universities to develop services science courses at more than 400 schools in 50 nations." It's clear that Palmisano understood that the shift would involve turning the company inside out, retraining employees, hiring new types of people, selling off unprofitable products (he sold the iconic PC group to Lenovo in 2005), and shifting the focus of M&A and R&D, effectively remaking everything from the ground up, including marketing. To that end, in 2008 Palmisano launched the company's famous Smarter Planet program, which showed the world the company had matured from making "dumb" hardware to investing in "smart" software and services.

An inadvertent DNA shift also can result from a change in leadership, which is what appears to be happening with Apple in the wake of Steve Jobs's death. For much of its life, Apple has been a Missionary, relentlessly seeking and then building the Next Big Thing—first with the Apple II, which put the company on the map, and then with Macintosh, the iPod, the iPhone, and the iPad. But few would argue against the consensus that Apple's releases and updates in the years since Steve's death in 2011 have lost their groundbreaking innovative fire. Tim Cook, Steve's handpicked replacement, has been an amazing steward of Apple's assets; he's nurtured them and grown them. But he has not been able to replace the visionary leadership of the company's founder. Not one single change-the-world product has emerged from the vault since October 5, 2011.

Take the Apple Watch. Released in April 2015, it was the first major product launched after Cook took over as the CEO. That means there was a lot of pressure on Apple to show the world that the company's Missionary status hadn't changed. According to James Titcomb of the *Telegraph*, the Apple Watch "was seen as a test of the company's ability to show it hasn't lost its mercurial founder's golden touch—the ability to create the thing that people don't know they need until they see it."

I like my Apple Watch just fine, but there's no getting around the fact that it doesn't do anything my phone doesn't do. Thus far it hasn't been a game changer. It hasn't been a category builder. Far from being the Next Big Thing, it's just another smartwatch, one among a recent wave of other such devices. As Dave Johnson of *CBS MoneyWatch* wrote, "Smartwatches have been vying for attention for a number of years now, but they've yet to go truly mainstream." No manufacturer, including Apple, he said, "has been able to tell a compelling story around wearable devices. . . . Certainly, there's a market for people who want smartphone notifications on their wrist, but average consumers would rather wear an inexpensive fitness band, it would seem, if anything at all."

Johnson notes that all the smartwatches recently released, including the Apple Watch, have featured "incremental refinements," which of course is the hallmark of a Mechanic. Whereas Missionaries are dedicated to creating groundbreaking change—to initiating a quantum leap in innovation—Mechanics are all about improving existing products. If you think about it, the Apple Watch is a lot like the Apple III computer, which was simply a better version of the Apple II. And that's just fine. People used the Apple III, and they use the Apple Watch. But no one walks around saying, "Wow! This Apple Watch changed my life!"

A smartwatch delivering only incremental improvements does not in and of itself topple Apple from its Missionary pedestal. Product failure—and the jury is still out on whether the Apple Watch is a failure—does not equate to a DNA change. Under Steve Jobs, in fact, Apple had plenty of failures. Lisa was a failure. NeXT was a failure. The Apple III was a failure (at least in the sense that it didn't expand significantly on the Apple II). Any company that stands the test of time is going to have many successes and failures in its product portfolio.

Nonetheless, the fact that the company has released products and updates featuring only incremental improvements in the years since the loss of its founder does suggest a loss of Missionary status, particularly in an industry focused unrelentingly on the Next Big Thing. As Farhad Manjoo wrote in his technology column for the *New York Times*, "Apple's view increasingly feels like an outdated way of thinking about tech." Commenting on the company's continued focus on physical devices, "expensive, perfectly designed, self-contained nuggets of aluminum and glass that you buy today, use for a couple years and replace," he noted, "Many of [Apple's] competitors have been moving beyond devices toward experiences that transcend them. These new technologies exist not on distinct pieces of hardware, but above and within them."

Natural Evolution

Wherever Apple ultimately ends up, it's important to note that many companies that start off as Missionaries do eventually become Mechanics—as is probably happening with Apple unless it manages to pioneer the Next Big Thing, and relatively soon. (Less common is the Missionary-to-Mother transition seen with Amazon, the Mother-to-Mechanic move of Wolfgang Puck, and the Mechanic-to-Missionary shift of Google.) Missionary-to-Mechanic is a natural evolution because in most cases the concept upon which the company was originally based was a sexy new product that resulted in industrywide changes and adaptations of human behavior. That clearly is the case with Apple. Transitioning Missionaries, particularly in the high-technology field, often already have the core DNA to be a Mechanic—many of their genes are Mechanic genes—and a large percentage of the pieces required to succeed as a Mechanic are already in place.

In any case, a change of DNA isn't necessarily a bad thing for Apple. It's been several years since the company lost its founder, and although it no longer enjoys the same staggering profit margins it enjoyed at its peak—from 2003 to 2016, Apple had 51 quarters of uninterrupted record-breaking growth in sales—Apple remains a strong company. Despite slowing sales, it boasts revenues and market share most companies would kill for. In fact, there's no reason Apple couldn't continue to be hugely successful as a Mechanic if it fully transitioned to one.

Without a new quantum leap innovation, however, it's hard to imagine that Apple will continue to realize the same levels of financial growth and prestige it enjoyed when it operated as both a Cult of Personality and a Next Big Thing Missionary. That said, it's too early to write Apple off in terms of being a Missionary. Apple being Apple—both culturally and financially—there are undoubtedly numerous projects in development throughout its vast South Bay complex. For example, the company appears to have as many as a thousand employees hard at work on a top-secret, next-generation "iCar," codenamed Project Titan, which, based on a rumored $10 billion R&D budget, presumably aims to alter our lives along the same lines as the iPhone once did.

And that's nothing to sneeze at. "My iPhone has become my social life and my career life," Akash Chudasama, an aviation and aerospace design strategist, told Kim Reynolds for an article that appeared in *Motor Trend* magazine about the Apple car. The reporter met with Chudasama and other transportation experts during a recent roundtable discussion at the ArtCenter College of Design in Pasadena, California, which Reynolds describes as home to a curriculum "so influential that it's essentially become the international epicenter of automotive design." Speaking of his iPhone, Chudasama said, "I don't really use [it] to make calls. I use it for everything else. So if [Apple] can make a telephone—something that's been around a hundred years—part of your way of life, what will they do with a car? . . . It'll be your entire way of life." He concluded by noting, "Traditionally your connection to a car is through its steering wheel; now it might be more about how the total transportation experience makes you feel."

Whether Apple releases a car (or any other future product) from the position of a Missionary or a Mechanic—or even at all—remains to be seen. But that uncertainty raises an interesting point: What exactly does it take to maintain Missionary status over the long term? Looking back at the histories of any number of Missionaries, from Apple to Alphabet and from Tesla to Virgin, the answer is clear: continual innovation. And not just the kind of innovation that results in a better mousetrap, but quantum leap innovation, the type that revolutionizes industries and changes human behavior.

It's Doable, but . . .

So yes, corporate DNA can be changed, but it isn't easy; nor in general, is it a good idea unless you have both unwavering vision and the capital to succeed. In any case, take a good hard look before you leap. And if you're falling rather than leaping, as in the case of an inadvertent DNA change, make sure you're heading in a direction you want to go. If you are not, take a page from the *Star Trek* crew's handbook and reverse engineer your way back to wherever, genetically speaking, you're meant to be.

When it comes to DNA, there are no half measures. You can't succeed in the market with the heart of a Mother if your company's core operates from the mindset of a Mechanic. Remember, DNA is the root of everything when it comes to competitive advantage, and operational alignment throughout the company, beginning with the C-suite, is imperative. Strategy, operations, sales, and marketing—all must reflect a company's genetic core. And in most cases, that core is fixed.

8

Cutting-Edge
Revolutions

In Chapter 4 we talked about category creation and whether creating a category requires that a company be a Missionary. (To recap: it doesn't; any DNA type can create a category or a subcategory.) The bigger issue, perhaps, and what many executive teams seem to be getting at when they push for Missionary status during the DNA exercise is what it takes to become the Next Big Thing regardless of whether a new category is created in the process. Sometimes the Next Big Thing and category or subcategory creation go hand in hand; other times they do not.

This chapter covers what it takes to create or develop the Next Big Thing—to shift human behavior on a large scale the way Henry Ford or Salesforce's Marc Benioff have done. It's no accident that many of these leaders are known for being charismatic and exhibiting a Cult of

Personality leadership that draws people in and compels them to follow wherever a leader decides to go. When you're building the Next Big Thing, it sometimes takes a big personality to push it out into the marketplace.

Those of us who worked with Steve Jobs experienced the power of his charisma and were driven to excel on his behalf. Although a charismatic leader is not a requirement for shifting human behavior, it certainly goes a long way toward achieving it.

No Guts, No Glory

It takes incredible guts and drive to turn your product or service into the Next Big Thing. More often than not, you're up against everybody telling you, "Stop wasting your time. It can't be done—there's absolutely no way it can be done." And sometimes they're right. There is no question that the innovation arena is filled with many more failures than successes, from the ventilated top hat to the electric pen and the flying car. Of course, today's failure is often tomorrow's success; that is why we'll probably see that flying car aloft before too much longer (though it seems likely that the window for the top hat and the electric pen has closed). As Thomas Edison said, "I have not failed 10,000 times. I've successfully found 10,000 ways that will not work." This is why Next Big Thing Missionaries often are run by strong-willed, never-say-never Cult of Personality types who have the force of will to soldier on in the face of relentless skepticism and sometimes outright hostility.

I vividly remember how many people were convinced that Steve Jobs did not have the technological know-how to rebuild Apple after his 1997 return to the company. Nonetheless, he revolutionized the world by building what he called "appliances" that enhance our lives. Of course, some of those appliances do more than just enhance our lives; in true Next Big Thing Missionary fashion, many have completely changed them. And few, perhaps, more than the iPhone. In an article for the *New York Times* about the demise of gadgets ("The Gadget Apocalypse Is Upon Us"), Farhad Manjoo notes that after nearly 40 years of abundance—"one gadget after another, from transistor radios to TRS-80s to Walkmen and Gameboys, then iPods and Flips, GoPros and Fitbits"—the golden age of gadgets appears to be coming to an end. He writes:

> Things were never easy for gadgets. The lives of gadgets have always been nasty, brutish and short. One year a gadget would be the Must Have of the Year, and the next year it would be old news. But that was the cycle, and it was fine, because there would always be another gadget.
>
> Then things got even worse. Suddenly, out of nowhere, the Thing That Does Everything emerged from Cupertino, Calif. That was almost 10 years ago now. You know what I'm talking about: the iPhone. We knew the Thing was going to be big, but we didn't know it would be this big. When the Thing threatened to eat up all the gadgets, nobody thought it would really happen. We still had hope that some gadgets would stick around.

In the end, however, Manjoo no longer shares that hope. Although the gadget marketplace has been a great laboratory, with gadgets feeding the "entire tech ecosystem with new ideas," because of the high cost of building hardware, the quick infusion of cheap knockoffs, and the short shelf life of must-have gadgets, the future looks grim for yesterday's gadgets. He concludes: "Now gadget riches for start-ups are no longer a regular mix of the tech business. The money is in finding ways to sell old stuff with new tech—what's the best way to deliver mattresses through an app?" It appears that the gadget of today is the smartphone app.

Having worked closely with Steve throughout his formative years, I can attest to the pull exerted by Cult of Personality Missionary leaders, their ability to inspire loyalty and drive change through sheer force of will. Here's how I described Steve in an essay I wrote for the *San Francisco Chronicle*: "If you were lucky enough to be on his team, it was because he needed your help. He made you feel that you were an important part of something much bigger than yourself—or even bigger than the company. With confidence in Steve's ability to do the impossible, we did not question anything he asked. We were young, exuberant and extremely inexperienced. He trusted us to perform miracles, and we simply did. Our limits were stretched right before our eyes, whether the request was filling a vase with fresh calla lilies in the middle of the night or writing software modifications to make Macintosh speak on the fly." The fact that we often had to put up with rude, even verbally abusive, behavior along the way was almost irrelevant. To work with Steve was to be as invested in the outcome as he was.

A strong character is often what it takes to elicit the best from employees and move a product or service successfully into the marketplace. Having a leader like Steve is generally a good thing, since Cult of Personality Missionary types do a better job than anyone else of making the impossible possible.

Or even to simply move an idea (or ideal) into the realm of possibility, no matter the consequences. Consider Elon Musk, who is using his Cult of Personality leadership to drive his biggest dream of all—colonizing Mars. In a headline for an article analyzing the feasibility of Musk's SpaceX plan to colonize Mars in the coming decades, Ars Technica characterized the tech mogul's Cult of Personality leadership in a nutshell: "Musk's Mars Moment: Audacity, madness, brilliance—or maybe all three" (a designation that could just as well suit any Cult of Personality Missionary leader). Describing Musk as a "dreamer" and a "true difference-maker," the article noted that his "evangelism about the colonization of Mars ... represents a huge gamble," both personally and for his company. "By putting his entire vision out for the world to see, Musk has emboldened his doubters ... And [he] may just be OK with that. SpaceX has always been a longshot."

In fact, Musk "had only given SpaceX about a 10 percent chance of 'doing anything.' Today they've upended the global launch business." (All this not too long after a ground test accident that resulted in the loss of the crucial Falcon 9 rocket—the second time in 15 months that SpaceX lost a Falcon 9. Although the explosion probably slowed the project's progress to some degree, industry experts reported soon afterward that the setback was unlikely to have a long-term impact on either SpaceX or the fledgling commercial space industry.)

The article concludes: "Musk's greatest attribute in an era of space timidity and a stagnated launch industry is probably this: he was never afraid to fail. In what may be his most revealing comment of all . . . [Musk] said, 'I just kind of felt that if there wasn't some new entrant into the space arena with a strong ideological motivation, then it didn't seem like we were on a trajectory to ever be a spacefaring nation, and be out among the stars.'"

Seeing the Possibilities

Although it sure helps, a Cult of Personality Missionary leader is by no means a *requirement* for launching the Next Big Thing. More than anything else, it all comes down to seeing the possibilities inherent in outlier behavior.

That is exactly what Reed Hastings did with Netflix. Although the company has transformed the way we watch TV, there was no guarantee Hastings would be the one to do it. People thought he was crazy when he split his company in two—Netflix for streaming content and Qwikster for the DVD mailing service—and opted to charge more for DVDs than for the streaming service. Customers thought he was crazy, too, and rebelled, in many instances canceling their subscriptions. Turning on a dime, Hastings killed Qwikster before it ever exited the gate and, as I wrote in an essay for the *San Francisco Chronicle*, "masterfully transitioned customer delivery from the U.S.

Postal Service to the Internet. It could have been a Kodak moment, but he fearlessly bet on the future and solved his innovator's dilemma in pretty short order."

Another leader who quietly overhauled the status quo to create the Next Big Thing was Oakland A's General Manager Billy Beane, who introduced the Moneyball system to major league baseball. Faced with a seemingly insurmountable financial disadvantage in selecting his 2002 roster compared with big-name (and big-pocket) teams such as the New York Yankees and Boston Red Sox, he tossed aside the subjective—and thus potentially flawed—beliefs and wisdom of managers, coaches, and scouts in favor of sabermetrics, an analytic, evidence-based system of measuring in-game activity. In short, the Moneyball method calls for using statistical analysis to allow small-market teams to compete against bigger teams by buying assets that are undervalued by other teams and at the same time selling players who are overvalued. Not every franchise has embraced the Moneyball system to the degree that Beane did, but his recruiting work-around put the 2002 A's back on the baseball map and forever changed the way baseball front offices look at their business.

Sabermetrics enthusiasts point to statistics-minded Theo Epstein, general manager of the 2004 World Series–winning Boston Red Sox and 2016 champions Chicago Cubs, as evidence that the method has permanently altered front-office decision making. Although Epstein is known to have focused heavily on player development and personnel management when putting together his organizations—particularly as sabermetrics moved into the baseball mainstream, thereby lessening its initial impact—there is little question that statistical reasoning played a role in the two long-suffering teams overcoming their respective 85-year and 108-year championship droughts.

No matter the leadership style, launching the Next Big Thing and changing the world (or at least the behavior of a portion of it) requires a leader with a unique perspective. It also necessitates an ability to inspire, the building of a support team, and complete, unwavering fearlessness. Wimps don't change the world.

Arrows in Their Backs

As far as category creation or becoming the Next Big Thing goes, however, here's the funny thing: it isn't usually a good idea to be first out of the gate. In fact, there's almost always a huge downside to it, particularly within the high-tech world. Why? Because whatever the industry, the pioneers are the ones facedown with arrows in their backs as others thunder past on their way toward Better Version 2.0. Pandora preceded Spotify and other streaming music apps; numerous search engines—beginning with the preweb Archie—paved the way for Google; and Myspace led the way before Facebook. All these first-out-of-the-gate companies introduced great ideas, but none was able to go far enough to change—much less revolutionize—behavior, at least not in the long run. Myspace and Facebook, for example, were founded on the same concept, but too much of the Next Big Thing equation was missing with Myspace, and part of that missing equation was Mark Zuckerberg's passionate leadership, which helped push Facebook to the forefront.

Steve Blank discusses this phenomenon in an article for *Fast Company*, noting that "Startups whose mantra is 'we have to be first to market' usually lose." Why? According to Blank, "First Movers tend to launch without really fully understanding customer problems or the product features that solve those problems. They guess at their business model and then do premature, loud and aggressive public relations hype and early company launches and quickly burn through their cash. This is a great strategy if there's a bubble occurring in your market or you are going to bet it all on flipping your company for a sale. Otherwise the jury is in. There's no advantage."

He points to Overture (originally GoTo.com) as an example. Considered the pioneer of paid search, Overture in 1998 created and demoed its pay-per-click search engine and advertising system at a TED conference. Two years later Google launched AdWords, its version of a pay-per-click advertising system, which allowed advertisers to create text ads for placement on the company's search engine. The outcome? Overture was acquired in 2003 for $1.6 billion by Yahoo!, its biggest customer. AdWords has evolved into the main source of revenue for Google, which is now worth more than $500 billion, a number that is expected to climb to $1 trillion by 2020.

One company that revolutionized an industry after a legal skirmish with a rival is Intuitive Surgical. Its robot-assisted da Vinci Surgical System, launched in 1999, improved on conventional laparoscopy, allowing surgeons to use robotics to operate through small incisions with greater precision, dexterity, and comfort. Surgical robotics has been around since the late 1980s—the industry developed from a desire to allow surgeons to operate remotely on soldiers wounded on the battlefield—but Intuitive Surgical has managed to make itself the big name in surgical robotics today. Although it was sued in 2002 by its earlier-out-of-the-gate rival, Computer Motion, Inc., for patent infringement of the ZEUS Robotic Surgical System, the two companies ultimately merged, and the ZEUS was phased out in favor of Intuitive Surgical's da Vinci.

This death-to-pioneers pattern has occurred across every industry I know. A visionary develops something new and cool (a lightbulb, an electric car, a portable phone, online shopping, robotic surgery, a streaming service), and very quickly others begin to parse it for mistakes and opportunities. Soon enough, by relying on innovative improvements, a financial edge, superior marketing, or legal maneuvering, Blank's Fast Followers overwhelm the First Mover, either absorbing or killing the original offering along the way. Innovator number two—or even number three or number four—then launches the "new" product or service into a large-scale success story, revolutionizing human behavior along the way.

Part II

Aha! in Action:
The Practice
of Positioning

What follows are six case studies of real companies that faced real positioning challenges in the real world. All are clients, so I know their trials and tribulations. We'll explore how two Mothers positioned themselves, one on Customer Experience and the other on Segmentation; how two Mechanics positioned themselves, one on Value and the other on Features; and how two Missionaries, one a Next Big Thing and the other a Cult of Personality, positioned themselves for market success.

9

Tile:
Delivering Peace of Mind

DNA: Mother

Genotype: Customer Experience

The Challenge: How to differentiate the company in an increasingly crowded market, how to connect better with customers, and how to establish leadership.

While writing this book, I took a trip to Tile, one of my favorite clients and the company behind the small square Bluetooth tracker and app of the same name that helps users find lost items. During my visit, I came across the following testimonial taped to the back of the stall door in the women's bathroom:

> My wife and I inherited a three-toed box turtle from our daughter when she moved away for college. Tippy resides

in a blue plastic tub most of the time, but my wife lets him out periodically to wander the first floor of our home. Thus he gets some much-needed stimulation and exercise. There is really only one catch. The one thing that turtles are really good at is hiding. So at the end of the day, as we head upstairs to bed, we would end our evening on hands and knees searching under chairs, sofas, and in every possible place a wayward box turtle might be concealed. It's a large house and the possibilities are numerous. So I purchased a Tile and, using adhesive putty, temporarily adhere it to his carapace when he is freed to roam. Locating him is now a simple and painless process.

Scroll through Tile's website and you'll find dozens of such testimonials: a six-year-old's beloved stuffed penguin retrieved in Times Square; a motorcycle recovered in San Francisco, 30 miles from where it disappeared; a laptop left on the roof of a car and later tracked to the side of a Minnesota highway, badly damaged but its hard drive intact enough to allow data and photo retrieval; keys plucked from the shallow waters off Long Island's Jones Beach after a half hour of submersion; a van stolen in Belgium that turned up in Holland; a wallet repossessed from a Barcelona subway-car pickpocket thanks to the "find me" button that set off a telltale alarm.

No wonder the company calls itself "The World's Biggest Lost and Found."

Tile's water-resistant tags use Bluetooth Low Energy to locate any item—wallet, phone, key chain, purse, laptop, gym bag, suitcase, bike—they're attached to. When a tagged object goes missing, the user fires up the Tile app; if the item is within a hundred feet or so, the app signals the Tile to beep. For an object that is farther away—even thousands of miles away—it provides updated coordinates for retrieval every time another Tile user passes the missing item with a mobile device, assuming that device is turned on. The Tile app runs in the background of users' phones, anonymously transmitting a signal to the Tile cloud and thus to the owner of the missing item. Each tag features a unique identification, though for security reasons no personal data are stored or transmitted.

Tile CEO and cofounder Mike Farley got the idea for the gadget after watching his wife, who he said is notorious for misplacing items, agonize in the wake of losing a family heirloom. That was when it hit him: everyone loses stuff. Everyone. Who hasn't experienced the frenzy of tearing apart the sofa in search of car keys or a mobile phone when rushing to get out the door? Or that gut-sinking feeling upon realizing that a bag, laptop, or bicycle isn't where it should be? "It was clear to us that this was a mass market problem," Farley said.

A mass market problem indeed. So much so that the company raised $2.6 million in its 2013 crowdfunding campaign—a record for Selfstarter, at least at the time—to fund the production of Tile's first-generation unit, far more than the $20,000 it was looking for and a significant step up from the $200,000 it received from Silicon Valley accelerator Tandem Capital, where Tile was incubated.

When we first met with Tile in 2013, it was working overtime to manufacture the product and meet the overwhelming demand from its crowdfunding campaign. At the same time, although thrilled by the response, it was frustrated by competitors clogging the space— some that had been in business longer than Tile and all producing what it considered inferior products—and wanted to better differentiate itself and broadcast its user-friendly features. "From the very beginning, our goal was to create a product anyone could use, from a 4-year-old to a 94-year-old," said Farley. "You don't have to be a tech person to use it."

Most of all, the company was eager to communicate the ability of the app to enhance lives and provide a better lifestyle. "We sold four and a half million Tiles over a period of 18 months," said Farley. "What are people doing with those Tiles? They're attaching them to the possessions they love."

How often do people lose their stuff? All the time, apparently. A Tile chimes every three seconds, according to the company, which means people are using the app to search for misplaced items 20 times a minute. And that doesn't take into account all the Tiles used to ring and find phones or those identified as lost, to be notified remotely via the Tile community. According to a survey of 2,000 British consumers age 16 and above conducted for Tile by Censuswide, an independent research company, 64 percent of people spend up to 15 minutes a day looking for their belongings—an approximation that adds up to more than 150 days over a 60-year lifetime. Considering the cumulative effects of wasted time, late departures, and short tempers that typically accompany frantic searches for missing items, the company wanted to showcase the sense of relief and the comfort that result from spending just 14 seconds on average to find an item tagged with a Tile.

The Aha!

The positioning and DNA exercises revealed that Tile's opportunity was not to be a rationally driven hardware product company. Instead, the company would be an emotionally driven software services company offering customers peace of mind. (It was clear to us from the get-go that Tile was a Customer Experience Mother.) First, however, it needed to overcome a public relations hurdle—and do it in a way befitting a Mother. Early on, while still building the device, Tile had accumulated a large community of people who had bought into the concept, paid for the device, and were growing impatient that they hadn't received it. (It was harder to manufacture and ship a new product than it initially appeared.) Chat groups mocking the company sprang up online, and angry e-mails flooded the company's San Mateo, California, headquarters.

New understanding of its DNA as a Customer Experience Mother, however, encouraged the company's management team to view its growing number of up-in-arms customers as a community even before the technology that enabled that community was up and running, and Tile began to incorporate community building into its daily business practices with regular communications and updates going out to the group. Not only was the outreach effort a success, serving to mollify exasperated customers, but reaching out to the community also laid the groundwork for future community-building initiatives, which have been key to the product's success.

Before long, with its production and shipping glitches remedied, the company delivered on the delayed Tiles and turned its full attention to its Mother role of delivering peace of mind to its customers. "Around here it really is all about the customer experience," said Farley, who regularly ticks off favorite stories of people who've posted online about their lost and found experiences—from an Alzheimer's patient who uses a Tile to keep track of his cane, thus granting him a degree of formerly lost independence; to the man who relied on the device to locate his wife in a crowded theater aboard a cruise ship; to the pet turtle highlighted at the beginning of the chapter, which still regularly disappears under a bed or couch or dresser but is now easily recovered within moments rather than hours. "We provide peace of mind to people and help them in a time of need, even panic," Farley said. "Again and again we hear from people that Tile has changed their lives."

Although Tile management ultimately came to embrace the Mother moniker, the team was initially dubious. "I grew up watching Arnold Schwarzenegger in movies like *Commando* and *Predator*," said Farley. "I loved the *Rocky* series. That's what I grew up on." Fast-forward to being the head of a technology company and, through the DNA positioning workshop, discovering that Tile was a Mother—a finding that was confirmed when the team settled on Caregiver during the Jungian archetype brand alignment exercise. Farley paused, recalling his uncertainty about the label. "Initially, it was like, really? Is that really the right thing?"

Embracing the Mother designation took time. "In my case there wasn't an immediate aha," Farley said. "It's just been a gradual process where I've really grown to believe that it's the right thing. To believe that a Caregiver is what we are. And as time goes on, I think that it makes more and more sense and that it's the right thing for us. We provide peace of mind to people. We help them in a time of need—and frequently in a time of panic. Tile is so much more than just a product. It's about making a difference to users, helping them aspire to a new lifestyle—to be 'a better you.'"

He noted that the hesitancy, even discomfort, he and the rest of the executive team initially felt about the Mother appellation occurred before Tile had shipped the product, before it began getting feedback that the device was improving lives. "We've actually heard that from a lot of people," he said. "They tell us this all the time: 'You guys have changed my life.'"

Although Farley and the rest of the leadership may not have experienced an immediate aha! about their Mother status, it was apparent to me and my colleagues early on in the DNA discovery process. Tile's concern with helping people in their hour of need; the emphasis on making the product so user-friendly that anyone could operate it; and its determination to make the product so cool and chic that, as Farley said, "a woman might put it on her purse even if it didn't do any-thing"—all pointed to Mother as the company's predominant DNA, with Customer Experience the obvious genotype. Even the crowd-funding video it put together in its earliest days focused on a positive user experience.

"I think when you look at Tile, the gut reaction is to think, 'Ah, it's a simple product,'" Farley said. "That's largely a result of how we've positioned it. We *want* people to think Tile is simple. But there are real complexities to the product, and the hardware is just the tip of the iceberg. We've got millions of Tiles on the network now, and there's a ton of software in the app for both Android and iOS. The analytics are massive—we have a giant analytics infrastructure built out for all portions of the user experience—which means there's a lot of data that we're going through every single day to provide a great customer experience."

Before we'd even defined Tile as a Customer Experience Mother, we worked with the management team to determine the criteria for the positioning exercise: a set of constraining parameters that the positioning statement should encompass and that we could check off at the end of the positioning exercise to ensure compliance (see Chapter 4). The team came up with the following:

- Emotional

- A solution to find your stuff

- (Life)style

- Elegant

- Simple

- Accessible

- Community-oriented

- Helpful

- Responsible/sustainable

All this led to the following positioning statement: *Tile is the first wearable for your things and is home to the world's largest community of people united in helping one another find their stuff.* Tile as a "wearable for things" is one of two key phrases in this statement. No other company in the space had claimed it. It was the empty spot on the map that Tile could fill, especially as a Mother. The second key phrase is "world's largest community of people united in helping one another find their stuff." This further differentiates the company with "world's largest community of people" serving one another in this way. The statement articulates the company's role and relevance with these two phrases.

Note the use of language in the positioning statement—the emphasis on humanity, on warm and fuzzy Mother-like words such as *home*, *community*, *united*, and *helping*. Tile's dedication to finding your personal things is written as an *experience*, a nurturing experience, as opposed to an impersonal announcement of capability. A Mechanic, for example, would never position itself along these lines. Instead, it might state, "We provide a tracking device for lost items that also tells you the time you lost the item and how long it will take you to retrieve it from where you are."

The elevator story we created for Tile expands on the idea of Tile as an emotionally driven software services company offering customers peace of mind: *Tile is the first wearable for your things and is home to the largest community of people united in helping each other find their stuff. Tiles are simple, sleek, and can be placed on valued things like keys, wallets, purses, computers, and luggage to make sure they can always be found. It's fun and easy to find your Tile by either seeing its last known location or asking it to beep. Tile community members are known for helping one another by passively creating local search parties that work together to find the stuff that somehow got away.* It also encompasses nearly all the criteria listed above. (Nine criteria is a lot; I generally recommend five to seven.)

One of the main reasons Tile contracted with us was for help in positioning itself to achieve its goals down the road—what I refer to as the bulk of the iceberg hidden beneath the waterline. In fact, it's important to understand that the Tile story outlined thus far is specific to the company at the time and that its positioning has evolved as the company has moved forward. "Our vision for Tile has been refined over the years," Farley said. "We now see a huge opportunity in location, which is why we are in the process of powering everything with smart location. When I look out three to five years, I see a world in which everything has a location built into it. Technically, it just makes sense. Ten years ago most people didn't even know what GPS was. Now we all have our smartphones, which have location built into them, and we live by them. Our tablets and our phones have the 'find my phone' functionality, and we love that too, right? In fact, 'find my phone' is the only way we find our tablets in a house with a bunch of kids! But we see location being built into other products as well. For example, anyone with a Tesla can open up the Tesla app and see exactly where their car is."

Farley anticipates that the company's software will be integrated into popular consumer electronics without the need to affix a Tile—items such as e-readers, smartwatches, wearable fitness trackers, and headphones. And that's just for starters. "Right now, maybe 0.1 percent of products have location built into them," he said. "I think there's probably about a trillion things on this planet that people want location built into. The numbers are mind-blowing. Our goal is to make Tile the solution that all those things run through for location."

Once again, Farley points to the beauty inherent in Tile's behind-the-scenes software. I think a common misconception is to think, 'Oh, Tile, the thing is so simple—location is just so basic,'" he said. "That's right, it is. It really is basic. It's a basic infrastructure that needs to be in place for a trillion different things. The number one thing that you get from having location in items you love is that you can find them. That's the first value we're providing to the customer."

Tile isn't alone in its belief that there's a big future in location. Byron Deeter, a partner at Bessemer Venture Partners, which led Tile's second-round financing in 2016 and ultimately helped raise $18 million (nearly double the company's 2012 series A round), told VentureBeat that "Smart location . . . has the potential to become the most valuable application for connected devices." In the same article, Farley predicted that by 2020 there will be 34 billion connected devices in the world, up from 10 billion in 2015. "We aim to give all of those connected devices—as well as the billions of analog items in the world—the power of smart location."

The Outcome

Cunningham Collective led the go-to-market strategy and execution for Tile's successful 2014 launch. We also led the creation of Tile's fund-raising materials and provided executive coaching, all of which helped secure Tile's $9.5 million series A financing.

By 2017 the company had sold more than 10 million Tiles, which are used to locate 2 million items in more than 200 countries each day. Tile already has begun to expand into the world of built-in location, partnering with Land Rover to integrate the tracker into the Discovery Sport's infotainment system. The technology allows customers to use the vehicle's touchscreen to establish a list of "essentials," which are automatically checked when the app is initiated. Passengers are also able to sound a 90-decibel alarm on the Tile tag to help locate any items lost within the vehicle.

When it comes to the future of location, there are countless roads Tile can travel. No matter where it goes, however, one constant is sure to remain: the extent to which Mother DNA is written into nearly everything the company does. "Knowing our DNA has helped shape our culture," Farley said. It shows up everywhere, including relying on "a gut check" when it comes to new hires to determine "whether or not we think this person is going to thrive in this environment and fit in with our Caregiver culture." It shows up in the company website and newsletters to the Tile community, which facilitate a sense of community through shared stories, ideas, and even a sense of fun: Farley noted that fans have sent in a number of creative videos about Tile, one of which featured users wearing Tile costumes. And it shows up in a feature embedded in the app that offers network users the option to anonymously—for safety reasons—thank one another for their help in recovering lost items simply by going about their daily business, with the app on their phones running unobtrusively in the background.

Over time, Tile has come to realize the extent to which the company's Caregiver vibe—its "Motherness"—has expanded to encompass the Tile community as well. "The interesting thing about Tile is that just by running the app, you're participating in the Tile community, you're being a Caregiver yourself," said Farley. "You're helping people. Only you can search for your Tiles—you can't search for anyone else's. But when someone reports an item missing and you walk by their Tile, you'll update its location. That person will get an update from our servers that says something like 'Hey, someone in the Tile community just updated the location on your Tile.' And then they have an opportunity to thank you."

Just as Mom would have you do.

Farley notes that the thank you messages Tile users extend to one another are a reflection of a practice initiated at the company in its earliest days. Each Friday, everyone in the company acknowledges someone for something he or she has done that week, anything from a pizza run to working overtime to debug a Bluetooth software problem. That was easy enough when there were only seven or eight employees; today, with nearly 10 times that many people in the office, it's not as simple. Nonetheless, Farley said, a modified version of the tradition continues, with employees continuing to write weekly notes, sometimes anonymously, acknowledging help offered and accomplishments achieved.

Indeed, a visit to the company's offices makes clear the extent to which Mother DNA has permeated the company dynamic. It even crops up in the women's bathroom, which on the first day I visited featured—in addition to the weekly updated customer experience testimonials taped to the backs of the stalls—a cloth towel, a colorful fabric rug, hand lotion, a lit candle, and a basket filled with feminine hygiene products.

How's that for a Mother's touch?

10

BuildingConnected:
Cutting Through the Noise

DNA: Mother

Genotype: Customer Segmentation

The Challenge: How to describe the company as a national player and illustrate its differentiation in the market.

The construction industry might be the last place you'd look to find a nurturing Mother, but when it comes to deliberating DNA—corporate or otherwise—you'd be wise to heed the old adage never to judge a book by its cover. (Advice, in fact, you may have heard first from your mother.)

A new player in construction bid management software—a specific and highly segmented industry—BuildingConnected was out to challenge a decades-old set of paradigms that dictated how general contractors and subcontractors communicate with one another. The San Francisco company, which launched in the fall of 2015, sought to differentiate itself in the market with its free and easy-to-use system, which allows general contractors to vet and prequalify potential subcontractors, send invitations to bid, and communicate directly with everyone on a project—messaging, sharing files, and getting proposals from subcontractors and vendors. BuildingConnected's system also enables owners to store and share documents, track the bidding process, and view project history and analytics.

The key factor here is that all bidding, communication, and tracking mechanics take place without anyone having to think about contact database management, a feature no other commercial construction software offers. "Think LinkedIn, but specific to the construction industry," said Dustin DeVan, the company's chief executive officer, who came up with the idea during the six years he spent in commercial construction with Bechtel, Rudolph & Sletten, and XL Construction before launching BuildingConnected. "The basic thesis is that everyone in commercial construction maintains a static contact database on everyone they know. It's like your Outlook. In commercial construction you maintain contact information on thousands of people. But people move around a lot, and so that information degrades over time. By building a network, it becomes like LinkedIn. You switch companies, you update your LinkedIn profile. That update then populates your entire network. You just communicate with people like you would send someone a Facebook message."

Although the long-term goal is to layer additional features onto its bid management solution to ultimately become a formal network operating system, BuildingConnected wanted to figure out the best way to talk about itself in terms of its current offerings. (You may recall the iceberg, introduced in Chapter 1, in which the exposed tip pinpoints a company's role and relevance in the next year or two and reaches only to spaces that it can own in the near term and thus is the focus of positioning.) DeVan knew he had a good product, and he knew where he wanted to take it down the road. For now, however, "We just wanted to know how to better express ourselves," he said. "Our question was, 'How do we describe ourselves so that people understand how we're different? How do we get across that we're not offering the same bid management solution as everyone else?'"

In short, they wanted to know how best to position BuildingConnected in the market. More specifically, they wanted to know how to position with an eye toward how that positioning might change over time in regard to the remainder of the iceberg, the unseen mass below the waterline (i.e., future goals and long-term vision).

At the same time, the company, even though it was working with some of the top builders in the industry—including Turner Construction Company, McCarthy Building Companies, Inc., Webcor Builders, and Skanska USA—also sought to overcome a perception that it was little more than a regional player that was not yet ready for prime time.

"That was something we really wanted to change," said DeVan. To that end, BuildingConnected wanted to reach a finite universe of general contractors—a thousand people in a few dozen markets—which would get the company to the point at which scale would become inevitable.

The Aha!

Although BuildingConnected's executive team initially was focused predominantly on branding needs—specifically, a website and a product marketing video—the leadership quickly recognized the importance of pinning down the company's precise strategic position and go-to-market strategy before focusing on the brand's creative expression.

"And that's when the fun began," said Zac Hays, the company's product manager, referring to our early meetings, during which we initiated the process of bringing the company's underlying DNA to light. Hays and DeVan agreed that the DNA exercise was particularly

eye-opening, with most members of the executive team initially seeing the company as a Missionary (as was noted earlier, nearly everyone in the technology industry starts out wanting to be a Missionary),
although Hays as the product manager, pushed hard for Mechanic. In
the end, however, the team was shocked to discover that it was actually a Mother—overwhelmingly so, in fact, in large part because of the
personality and concerns of its CEO.

Here's how it unfolded. During a meeting between my team and
the BuildingConnected C-suite, the executives learned that a customer had called in with a concern about vendors. "Everyone dropped
whatever we were doing to attend to the problem," Hays recalled.
"Dustin jumped up and said, 'I'm calling this guy right now.' And
your team is like, 'Hmmm, the CEO is interrupting our meeting to
call a single customer in Texas. One customer is having a minor issue
and the whole team just drops everything and runs off to deal with it.
Interesting . . .'"

It was immediately apparent—to my team, anyway, if not yet
to theirs—that BuildingConnected was a Mother and that it was a
Mother focused on taking care of a particular market with a specific
need. For this reason, we genotyped the company as a Segmentation
Mother rather than a Customer Experience Mother. However,
just as many Missionary companies take advantage of both Cult of
Personality and Next Big Thing, Mother companies take advantage
of both Segmentation and Customer Experience, with one genotype
standing out a bit more than the other.

"Our true colors showed through that day," said Hays, referring
to the interrupted meeting, "although it took us a while to accept and
then embrace it. The last thing most of us wanted was to be a customer
company. 'Mother' just didn't seem to fit our image."

But embrace it they did . . . eventually. The turning point came
at our next meeting while we were revisiting an earlier discussion of
the 12 Jungian brand archetypes (covered in Chapter 5). At some
point, after much discussion, "Most of us in the room were leaning

toward the Hero archetype," Hays said. "There was a sense of 'We want to fight against bad software and everything else that was bad in the industry—to fight for change on behalf of our clients.'" Then DeVan laid two cards on the table: the Caregiver and the Lover. At first everyone laughed—DeVan is a big guy both in size and in personality; it's clear that he knows his way around a construction site. Soon enough, however, his choices began to make sense and no one was laughing anymore.

"That's how we think about everything: we're always looking for what is the best solution for the customers," said Hays. "We want to make sure they're happy. You guys said, 'Just look at the feedback you're getting from your customers.' It was all about how customer service was great, how great the experience was. You told us, 'This is what you guys do every day. Every product that you run, you're talking about the user experience. You're not asking, How can we hit different price tiers? Or any other product-oriented question.' Once we got that, it was like, yes, we really do care about our customers and the user experience they have—more than anything on the product side. We don't have a suite of products. We have one cohesive solution."

Hays said that it was helpful that each management team member was required to choose an archetype independently before sharing the pick with the group, since initially few of the executives overlapped in their choices. Looking at one another's cards during the first round resulted in "a little bit of shock," he said; the group's picks spanned the spectrum from Hero to Sage. As a team, it was clear that they weren't working from the same page.

Talking through why they chose the archetypes they did was a learning experience, Hays said, and in time he and the other Mechanic and Missionary holdouts came to embrace DeVan's Caregiver pick, which aligns with being a Mother in terms of the DNA methodology. (Although at first glance DeVan's second choice, the Lover, initially struck the group as humorous, the archetype's commitment to intimacy and relationships is also consistent with Mother DNA.) It also explained why so many of them were drawn to the Hero archetype. "I really felt, 'Oh, we're fighting for something,'" Hays said. "But it wasn't until we were looking at these cards that we realized what we were fighting for. We're not fighting against competitors or against 'the Man.' We're fighting for our customers, for people who really need some help getting technology embedded into their industry. They're great, smart people who have been building amazing buildings for decades. But sometimes technology moves in a different way, a different style than they're used to, and it's our job to help them."

DeVan agreed, noting that "Silicon Valley produces the best technology in the world" but hadn't focused much on the construction industry until recently. "Well, guess what? It takes a while for any industry to adopt technology, so we can't expect [contractors] to ramp up overnight."

As he warmed to his subject, DeVan's Mother DNA was on full display. "Some of my peers who are CEOs or CTOs or in charge of other construction technologies make fun of construction," he said. "They say, 'Oh, well, they're not sophisticated. They're not used to technology.' That's not true at all. Our customers are very sophisticated. Just look at the structures they put together; they're incredibly complex. You don't build a $2 billion project like the one downstairs"—referring to a neighboring construction site—"and not have a high level of sophistication. Just because they aren't the best with a particular application or they don't use a computer, that does not make someone unsophisticated. I hate that preconceived notion."

But it was exactly because the construction industry was late to the technology game and slow to embrace it that the Mother in BuildingConnected put so much effort (even if unknowingly) into making its free platform easy to use—including by automatically updating users' contact databases—and then backed that platform with responsive customer and tech support.

With that understanding, it was just a short step to putting together BuildingConnected's positioning (construction bid management with a refreshingly different experience) and the elevator story:

> BuildingConnected is a construction communication platform with a refreshingly different approach. It's ridiculously easy to use. It's free to find, communicate, and share documents with general contractors and subcontractors securely. Its analytics help everyone get smarter every time they work together. And you never have to update a contact database again. It's about time.

Looking back, one of the exercises DeVan said he appreciated most was seeing BuildingConnected placed within Steve Blank's petal diagram (introduced in Chapter 4), which offered a wide-angle lens on competitive differentiation. The diagram, he said, did a great job of mapping the landscape of the construction industry by showing the team the space BuildingConnected inhabited, identifying where competitors and those in neighboring industries fell on the diagram, and encouraging the company to consider where it might want to extend its reach. It also offered the C-suite a reminder that it needed to consider the possibility that many of the companies inhabiting other petals were equally determined to extend their reach and might set their sights on muscling in on BuildingConnected's territory.

The Outcome

Post-aha! positioning included helping BuildingConnected zero in on the focused differentiators and reasons to believe that would move its initial target audience to think differently—all without overwhelming existing customers with change. It also helped the company evolve its go-to-market approach as early adoption conversions tipped into the scale stage.

With a new position, brand, marketing plan, and website, BuildingConnected reached its goal of more than a thousand general contractors across dozens of markets using the platform by the end of 2016. That made the company the largest provider of bid management services.

The impact of DNA-based positioning extends well beyond the numbers, however. "We consider position in all of our designs—the issue is whether or not they're 'refreshing,'" said Hays. "It becomes a filter for everything we do. We even talk about it: 'Is this pricing model refreshing?' And often we're like, 'No, it's actually kind of annoying.' Other times we'll look at the design and say, 'Yeah, it works, but it's just not refreshing. Back to the drawing board.'"

DeVan points to the link between DNA type and positioning and the effectiveness of the latter growing out of the former. "I think it works in combination with the great people we hire, but our positioning statement has definitely been key because we are growing faster than any other software provider in commercial construction," he said. "And that's even with a team that's much smaller than most of our competitors. Everyone here knows now that they need to talk to customers."

DeVan laughed, noting that he has an unusual "problem" for a technology company: Hays, as product manager, "spends almost too much time on customer support." (Imagine the CEO of a Mechanic ever saying that.) He acknowledged, however, that he's no different. "Back when we were a really small team, I was almost OCD when it was just me managing support. I just can't stand not to respond. In my experience, there's nothing worse than e-mailing a company for support and then they don't get back to you for three days. I'm like, 'Why did that take so long?' It all adds up to a terrible customer experience." In the end, he said, talking to customers is simply good business. "If you're a customer company and you really provide a great experience, that pays dividends. Customers become loyal, and when they do, it's going to be very, very hard to pull them away."

The biggest upside of all that hands-on involvement with customers, Hays said, is how much it informs product development. "Probably 99 percent of our product decisions come directly from something happening with the customers," he explained. DeVan agreed, adding that he encourages all employees, particularly the sales group, to review the customer support team's reports periodically. "It gives everyone an understanding of where the pain points are."

Keeping an eye on those pain points also serves to reinforce the company's DNA-based positioning. "We have grown a lot since we started the [DNA] exercise," said DeVan, both in size and in understanding what the company is trying to accomplish. As such, "we need to make sure everyone in the company understands that these are our values and that we think these values and this position are going to be really successful in driving customer adoption." The same goes for all new employees, no matter the division. "Everyone gets the same message: We're a customer company, and this is what that means to us. This is our culture. This is our philosophy."

In fact, knowing the company is a Mother has made a big difference in streamlining the hiring process, according to Hays. "If we feel like someone's philosophy is not going to align with ours, that person won't be hired. If we're looking for our next product manager and someone comes in who really likes the Microsoft model of 'fill a bunch of segments with a bunch of products and then fix them later'—well, that's probably not going to jibe with the way we work."

BuildingConnected's "refreshing" campaign has been a hit in its industry and has enabled it to meet its new-business goals within the allotted time frame. But that business success stems directly from its success in distilling the company's DNA-based positioning throughout the organization before sending that message out into the market. Internal alignment across all departments around its Mother-based position—"BuildingConnected offers a refreshingly different, ridiculously easy experience"—ensured cohesion in external storytelling.

The executive team's excitement about that alignment hasn't abated. Hays is particularly pleased with the impact it's had on the technology branch of the company, which is composed of a population known for its cynicism in the face of messaging and marketing. "We had a big release a couple of weeks ago that customer feedback was mixed on," he said. "All the engineers were working all night to get through all the feedback because everyone knows that the customer response is the most important thing. Even though we weren't launching anything new, everyone knew the most important thing was to get back to those customers [who] had complained and solve their issues so that we could move forward. It was a crazy week.

"Some companies would just say, 'Eh, whatever. We'll fix it on the next release. Those customers aren't going to leave us. Let's just get another feature out there.'" Hays speaks from experience, having worked for Microsoft during its Vista launch, where he said that was a common attitude. "People would say, 'Oh, we'll get it right next time.' Our attitude here is, 'No, we'll get it right *this* time.'"

11

Addepar:
Weapon of Choice

DNA: Mechanic

Genotype: Value

The Challenge: How to articulate the value of real-time data mining for an industry stuck in its ways.

A 2015 Deutsche Bank report estimated the value of the global market for financial assets—stocks, bonds, and any number of securities—at nearly $294 trillion. No surprise, then, that the "finance sector spends more on technology, as a proportion of its revenues, than any other industry," according to *The Economist*. "Nevertheless," the article continued, "compared with the world of e-commerce, banking still sometimes gives the impression of a Volkswagen Beetle instead of a Formula 1 racing car."

Silicon Valley's Addepar Inc. is working overtime to bring the finance sector up to twenty-first-century speed. It offers a cloud-based platform for the global wealth and investment management market that enables financial and wealth managers to be more agile and transparent with their clients, which include family offices, registered investment advisors (RIAs), foundations and endowments, global advisories, banks, financial services firms, and wirehouses.

The company, which in addition to its Mountain View, California, headquarters, has offices in New York, Chicago, and Salt Lake City, launched in 2009 in the wake of the previous year's financial crisis. According to CEO Eric Poirier, who took over management of the company in 2013, that crisis—among a myriad of other things—"demonstrated that a lot of large investors with complex portfolios had way less of an understanding of what they actually held and what they were exposed to than they might have thought otherwise."

Poirier got his start in the financial world just out of college in 2003 when he joined Lehman Brothers, where for the next three years he worked in fixed-income analytics and wrote many of the tools depicted in the book and movie *The Big Short*. What struck him most, he said, was that Lehman was spending $4 billion a year on technology. "But when they referred to technology," he said, "that really meant people—people using old systems. From my perspective as a programmer, I realized we could do a lot better."

Legendary tech entrepreneur and billionaire venture capitalist Peter Thiel, a mentor since Poirier's college days, lured him across the country in 2006 to serve as a director at Palantir Technologies, a computer software and services company specializing in big data analysis, which Thiel had cofounded in 2004 with four others, including the serial entrepreneur Joe Lonsdale, who later would go on to cofound Addepar. Poirier and Lonsdale worked closely together at Palantir, where, Poirier said, "we got good at building large-scale modern technology to pull data from a whole bunch of different places, unify it in one data model, and then build intuitive tools on top of that." After nearly seven years at Palantir, the last few dedicated to building the commercial side of the business, Poirier joined Lonsdale at Addepar, having realized that he "wanted to get back to where technology intersected with the heart of the financial system."

Poirier describes Addepar as purpose-built technology for investment and wealth managers to pull together in one central place all the information about complex investment portfolios, provide intuitive tools that enable them to slice and dice those portfolios, and then succinctly outline the details of those portfolios. "Many of our clients are high-end wealth managers," he said. "They provide a white-glove service to their clients, making them—essentially—relationship managers. Which means they need great technologies to enable them to tell each client a clear story and tell it in a way that's tailored for that specific client. We're offering a better set of tools so that they can better serve their clients."

Addepar does that by providing interactive analysis that renders complex portfolios easy to understand. "If I'm a client of a wealth manager, the plain-English questions I want answers to are 'What's my net worth? How are my assets allocated, and how does that vary across accounts? How many funds am I invested in? How are the funds doing? How exposed am I to whatever's going on this week with Apple? I saw this weird thing happen with crude oil. How did that affect me?'"

There's a problem, however: "When you start asking these questions, more often than not an advisor says, 'I'll get back to you in a week or two.' But what that advisor really means is, 'I live in an Excel world and I'll have to do all this stuff manually by pulling data out of old accounting systems.' What we're doing is using technology to solve problems that for the last few decades have required manual effort."

Addepar's platform brings a simpler, more commonsense approach to investing, Poirier said, one that has been lost as the investing world has become increasingly complex. "You might think, 'Well, of course that technology already exists.' Because it does exist—in different forms—on Google and Amazon, but what you'd find is that it doesn't exist in the financial world. So many investment dollars have been poured into building technology within banks. But each of those banks has technology that's basically locked within a walled garden; the technology isn't shared by other banks."

And that, from an investor standpoint, makes things complicated. "If you have accounts at three different banks and you have investments in a bunch of different funds, what you end up with is a zillion different data formats for receiving information," Poirier said. "As a result, you need to have a whole bunch of people on hand every single day to make sense of each of those formats to try to figure out how it all fits together."

That is why Addepar took on the task of integrating the banks' old data systems and transforming the data into one model. "Say you've just decided to allocate 20 percent of your portfolio to Latin America," said Poirier. "Our model shows you the various things that you can invest in Latin America. It shows you the trade-offs in terms of the return profile of this investment versus that one. And that fee that you're going to pay to get into this investment versus that one. Over time we can help people understand, 'Okay, if you're trying to get this type of exposure, doing it the way you're doing it, you're paying five times too high a fee. To accomplish the same goal, you could just as well have bought this other investment and paid a much lower fee.' It's all a matter of being able to navigate the entire financial world in a way that's internally consistent."

Simply put, the financial world was stuck in an outdated, error-prone, and byzantine process that relied predominantly on people using 30-year-old software and thumbing through reams of spreadsheets (i.e., combing through static data and doing work that technology can do better and faster). Addepar modernizes the experience, with advisors drawing data directly from banks over fully secure and encrypted channels—Poirier describes the technology as "industrial strength plumbing"—thus enabling wealth managers to answer clients' questions instantly using only a single computer or tablet. "Rather than waiting to get a report every month or so, the clients get a real-time look at exactly where their investments are and how they're doing."

Poirier likens Addepar's model to an iPhone, which allows access to any number of apps without the user having to worry about how the data are stored; Apple's mobile operating system has it handled. "For us, it's kind of the same concept," he said. "We've taken on the heavy lifting of pulling together all the data from the various banks, and we've set up the right security permissions and algorithms to deliver real-time information from across a variety of sources, making it possible for our customers to interact with the data, conduct scenario planning, and have timely discussions with their clients about investment decisions. In addition, if our customers want to bring to market a new risk model or new financial products, we make it easy for them. We provide the underlying data access and modeling, enabling them to develop tools on top. It's a matter of being much more thoughtful about the various parts of the financial system and how to codify them in a way that's intuitive."

That may sound easy enough in today's engineering world, he said, but from a data standpoint—a technology standpoint—scaling it for user experience was challenging. "We've taken an ambitious approach just in building the technology itself and then positioning it in the market to people who have been living in Excel for decades."

With a mission to solve the challenges of modern investment management and reconceptualize what technology can do to bring the financial industry more in line with the modern world—the world of Google and Amazon—Poirier and his leadership team understood that the company needed to build momentum around its fit in the market in a way that ultimately would establish Addepar not only as a leader in financial technology but also as the future of the industry. To achieve that leadership and promise, it also sought to create a brand that would appeal to top technology talent—potential hires.

Customer interviews we conducted as part of our research for Addepar revealed that the company was perceived as a weapon for investment managers to deliver a step change in decision making for their clients. But how that weapon worked wasn't readily apparent, especially to established old-school investment firms that were used to working in a relatively low-tech, often disorganized environment—basic Excel rather than Olympic-level programming. "We understood the need to clearly articulate our identity," Poirier said, "and were looking to operationalize our culture and vision in a way that would make them tangible to the outside world—to communicate so people can understand what we do." In essence, he said, "Addepar was long on R&D and short on communication."

The Aha!

As always, our first task was to work with the leadership to determine Addepar's core DNA. Although the company's game-changing data-mining and interactive platform initially led the management team to toy with the idea of positioning the company as a Missionary—several members were drawn to the Magician card when they were exploring Jungian archetypes during the brand portion of the workshop—the exercise ultimately revealed that Addepar was a Mechanic. Although Missionary certainly makes up more than a few strands of Addepar's DNA, it soon became clear that the firm is driven predominantly by engineering and technology with a customer experience that is reliant on its ability to provide a superior product (i.e., one that simplifies sophisticated portfolio access for investors and advisors and gives them real-time access to investment information), not customer service. In true Mechanic fashion, approximately half of Addepar's 250 employees are either engineers or data scientists. Further, among those 250 employees, just 4 are salespeople. According to Poirier, most customers discover Addepar via word-of-mouth referrals—yet another indication of Mechanic status. Bottom line: the company wins in the marketplace through a better product with better performance than the status quo. "Build a good product and people talk," he said.

Additional discussion also revealed that the idea of redefining money management—a Missionary undertaking—wasn't likely to appeal to the outside world. The finance industry is notably conservative, and any disruption would be likely to instill more trepidation than excitement.

Thus far, all fairly straightforward. As was determining that the company offers its customers value (its Mechanic genotype) thanks to a technology platform that sifts through large data sets to extract patterns and trends that were previously inaccessible. Just as Waze mines and prioritizes traffic data to offer the best route to circumvent an accident snarling the road three miles ahead, Addepar mines big chunks of data to bypass outdated and expensive manual processes to expose information that provides investors with immediate and valuable insight.

The next step was to determine the Criteria, the agreed-upon parameters put forth by the management team, which would both encompass and constrain Addepar's position as well as let the group know when they'd landed on it. In the end, the management team decided on just two criteria.

- Balance today's appeal with tomorrow's promise

- Attract and energize investors and potential hires

What really changed the conversation for Addepar, however, was the first of the two Criteria, the idea of being the future of something that already exists. Addepar could, of course, create a new category for financial investing, but the wealth management industry was crowded enough. Not to mention that the introduction of something "new" to a traditional industry wasn't likely to be a winning strategy. Just as with the publishing industry, which was late to the digital revolution, change comes slowly to the finance sector, and not everyone in wealth management is ready to embrace the big data approach.

Smart investors, however, *are* ready, and if your company is the future of something—of anything; it doesn't matter which industry—forward-thinking people who are focused on that something will want to talk to you. All of which led us to the conclusion that highlighting Addepar's ability to bring something new to the realm of wealth management software—its ability to supply valuable insight previously unavailable to the market—was the very thing that would secure its position as the industry's future.

And the future Addepar has in mind? "What we really want is to be the operating system for the global financial system," Poirier said. Visit the company's website and you'll find that positioning front and center. Today's appeal: "Addepar is the first investment management platform that easily handles all of your assets, connecting your financial goals and objectives with real world actionable insights." Tomorrow's promise: "Explore the new operating system for our financial world."

Articulating a broad product vision that works today and into the future is what Mechanics like to do. And for this Mechanic, the product-laden positioning statement does just that.

The Outcome

Clarifying Addepar's position in the market contributed to a $50 million series C raise in 2014. (In June 2017 the company concluded a series D funding round that pulled in an additional $140 million.) In the wake of the series C financing, Addepar has positioned itself as a solution for today's investor and developed a concise corporate narrative that is focused on key messages that have been tested in the market (integrity, transparency, and impact). Ultimately, Addepar's high-quality, product-centric DNA became the bridge to a corresponding brand that appeals to customers and potential hires both in Silicon Valley and on Wall Street.

With an eye toward ensuring that the foundation of that bridge remains strong, in March 2014 the company cohosted the world's largest competitive hackathon in history, followed by a second hackathon two years later. In keeping with Addepar's Mechanic DNA, open-to-the-public hackathons are about not only improving the product but also attracting the attention of Silicon Valley's brightest technology minds. "Hackathons are really important to our culture," said Poirier. "They are a great way to reinforce our commitment to engineering." They're also a great way to put Addepar on the map and attract engineering talent beyond Silicon Valley's borders. "A lot of the folks who compete in the hackathons are from outside the United States. They broaden our identity in those markets where we really haven't made a concerted effort in recruiting."

Internal hackathons are equally important to cementing Addepar's culture, he said, and take place every three to six months. Programmers present to their peers, who then vote to determine the winner. Poirier chooses the prizes, which are generally experiential and have featured field trips to innovative companies such as the Tesla factory just across the bay and SpaceX, which is outside Los Angeles.

Although Addepar's overwhelming focus on technology ensures its Mechanic status, it is important to note that both its identity and the groundbreaking nature of its data-driven technology platform are built in large part on the company's supporting Missionary DNA. And although that DNA may continue to play a secondary role in the company's future as it looks to expand both overseas and further into different market segments—including endowments, foundations, pensions, and sovereign wealth funds, all of which entail working with complex portfolios, it also means that a DNA change down the road isn't out of the question.

Again, it's an issue of what the iceberg that remains beneath the waterline keeps hidden. Addepar is built on an open platform; anyone can build on top of it. It's an attitude entirely in keeping with a company determined to be the "operating system for our financial world."

"Looking out 10 to 20 years, that's where the longer-term opportunity lies," Poirier said. "In order to achieve a broader transformation, we're building a product that's designed to be a really sharp wedge in the financial services world."

By virtue of leading with tech, he said, "we're able to organize something that used to be really disorganized. Once it's organized, you can do any number of new things. It's basically a matter of building out scaffolding. Once you have your scaffolding in place, you can build a foundation. And then once you have a sturdy foundation, you can build new material on top of it. This is how your Googles and Facebooks and Amazons can bring new products to market and open up totally new industries—they're building on top of a foundation that didn't exist before. It's the same thing with financial services. You've got some hundred-odd trillion dollars in assets but no common platform. You have stock exchanges and you have big banks, but they're really all discombobulated. It's just a bunch of people all shoveling information and pitching different things, but it doesn't hang together. What we're doing is building the foundation so we can all hang together."

For now, however, Addepar is content to position itself as a Value Mechanic. "We've been really consistent with our identity as a product company," Poirier said. "We pushed ourselves to envision what the financial system would look like with one really well built, highly configurable, and highly customizable product that you can push into $120 trillion of assets," complete with a back end that unifies everything.

"I think we've hit that inflection point where it's become a standard for certain pockets of the industry," he said. "At this point, if you don't have it and everyone else does, you're at a disadvantage." He concludes with an analogy that mirrors the one *The Economist* used in the article quoted at the beginning of this chapter: "If you're still riding your horse and everyone else is flying by in their Ford, you're behind."

12

Synaptics:
The Human Interface
Revolution

DNA: Mechanic

Genotype: Features

*The Challenge: Positioning for new relevance in the
semiconductor industry.*

I n the spring of 2016 Synaptics Incorporated, a company founded in
1986 by two engineers deeply interested in the intersection of neural
networks and technology applications, celebrated its thirtieth year in
business. The founders applied the neural network concept to transis-
tors on chips and built a touch-sensing interface solution that became
the first touchpad, a technology that was widely adopted throughout the computer industry, so widely, in fact, that Synaptics became
known as "the touchpad company."

Needless to say, its thirtieth anniversary was a really big deal for the San Jose–based company. Sure, plenty of organizations can point to a longer pedigree; DuPont, Colgate-Palmolive, and Macy's, for example, have all been in business for more than 150 years. And then there's Japan's Nishiyama Onsen Keiunkan, a family-run inn that was founded in AD 705 and is the world's oldest company, still going strong 52 generations later. The hotel, situated at the edge of a hot springs in the southern Japanese Alps, is a longevity outlier, of course, but according to the World Economic Forum, the average life span of a multinational, Fortune 500–size corporation is 40 to 50 years. Still, the fact that many companies last long enough to celebrate their golden anniversaries does nothing to negate Synaptics' three-decade achievement. As CEO Rick Bergman wrote in a blog post commemorating the milestone, "Thirty years is a long time by nearly any measure, but it's practically an *eternity* in the technology world."

The company's 30-year tenure is remarkable for another reason as well. "We're the last American company standing in our field," said Bergman, noting that all of Synaptics' competitors today are based in Europe and Asia. As the last American company in this space, Synaptics is clearly doing something right. Bergman, who graduated from the University of Michigan the year Synaptics was founded and joined the company as CEO in 2011, attributes this longevity largely to its steadfast commitment to its core values, the first of which reads: We value innovation, and we innovate to win. "Innovation lives within everything we do," Bergman said. "It's woven into absolutely everything we do. Simply put, we make devices easier to use. That was the message we wanted to get out."

At the same time, Synaptics knew that if it wanted to remain standing in an increasingly global competitive environment—and, in fact, lead the way—it needed to define its position in the marketplace better, particularly in light of recent innovations and acquisitions in areas such as display drivers, touch and display integration, and biometrics. Known predominantly for its work in developing the touchpad, the company was eager to establish itself as the innovator it was across a wide range of human interface solutions (the sort of technology that struck audiences as almost unimaginably futuristic in the 2002 movie *Minority Report*), including mobile computing, entertainment, automotive, and other consumer electronic developments. In short, it wanted out of the touchpad "box" it increasingly found itself locked in, particularly in a world in which touchscreens increasingly are coming to be seen as the norm. "I'd mention the name Synaptics," Bergman said, "and everyone would say, 'Oh, right, you're the touchpad people.' I got that all the time."

There was a second hurdle to surmount as well. Although Synaptics knew it excelled at innovating, too often those innovations never saw the light of day—or if they did, they were snapped up by competitors who took the company's creativity to the next stage. "A passion for innovation is great," said Bergman. "But we aren't here to innovate for fun or for innovation's sake. We're here to make money." He recalled meeting with the company's board of directors during his hiring process and hearing one of the members remark that Synaptics was great at finding veins of gold but not at getting that gold to the surface. The company would invest time and money in innovation only to see other companies scoop up its products and walk away with the commercial success. Now, however, the company was ready to showcase its innovative products and abilities: everything from biometric sensors for the automotive industry to secure fingerprint authentication across multiple markets. After years of conservative operation, it was time to take risks and in doing so get what Bergman calls "the good stuff" out of the lab and into the market.

The Aha!

When we first met with Synaptics in 2014, the company knew it should be positioned in the human interface space in which it already was operating. The management team wanted help defining that position to bring the concept of human interface to life and place Synaptics in the lead role.

No matter what stage of the positioning game a company is in when we meet, our first task, of course, is to determine its core DNA. Despite a brief flirtation with Missionary status—an almost obligatory rite of passage for many technology executives when we explain genetic positioning—it was quickly apparent that with over 1,900 patents either pending or issued and with the fact that 70 percent of Synaptics's 1,850 employees work in technology, engineering, and product-design functions, Synaptics was a poster child for Mechanic DNA. More specifically, it was a Mechanic dedicated to offering its customers a wide variety of features, all with an eye toward enhancing user experience. "Computers, smartphones, tablets, and cars don't need more gigahertz or megabytes," Bergman wrote in his thirtieth-anniversary blog. "Rather, because of their complexity, they need to be conceptualized and designed through a user experience lens."

To that end, Synaptics has consistently added to its product line over the years, moving from notebook PCs into mobile and then adding display drivers, fingerprint sensors, and a myriad of other technologies to its offerings. Notably, it also has continued to update the original touchpad. "We've been innovating touchpad technology for over 20 years now," Bergman said. "Some people say, 'It's just a boring old touchpad; why bother?' But if you tried to use a touchpad from 20 years ago, you'd think, 'Forget it.' That's true even of a touchpad from 5 years ago." Bergman points to one of the company's biggest and most recent innovations where the touchpad is concerned: palm rejection algorithms that virtually eliminate accidental selection for a hand resting on a notebook PC. "Once you get used to the technology and you sit down in front of something that doesn't have it, you think, 'What the heck? Why is my cursor going all over the place?' It's that kind of innovation that always keeps us ahead of the folks that try to clone us or the other big semiconductor companies we competed against that didn't use user experience to drive their vision. They wouldn't see those things. They'd opt for something that was a little faster or a little cheaper, but they'd miss the boat on what was really important: user experience. We're constantly iterating to improve user experience."

That constant iteration to improve an existing product incrementally is exactly what makes Synaptics a Features Mechanic (as opposed to a Value Mechanic such as Addepar). Of course Synaptics offers its customers value—just as Addepar offers its clients plenty of features—but the company's drive to innovate continually on features is a dead giveaway to its genotype. "Ours is a tinkerer culture," said Bergman. "If you walk into offices around here, you'll see a bunch of old devices lying around, different things people have worked on over the years. There's an attitude here that lends itself to innovation."

An added twist is that in working to deliver an intuitive user experience, Synaptics doesn't innovate just for itself. Instead, it brings its technology to its partners, who then decide what to do with it. More specifically, Synaptics innovates in conjunction with those partners—be they Mothers, Mechanics, or Missionaries—and in doing so empowers them to adapt the technology to their own specifications before production. In short, Synaptics empowers its partners to deliver intuitive user experiences.

For example, say I'm a big restaurateur in the middle of designing my new dream restaurant that I plan to open in Silicon Valley. Because my restaurant will sit in the heart of the world's most famous tech universe, I've decided that in addition to having great food prepared by a celebrity chef (my restaurateur fantasy has no limits, financial or otherwise), I want it to be seen as modern and cool—the epitome of cutting edge. That means it must feature the highest technology the Valley has to offer, starting with a state-of-the-art interface for ordering food. To that end, I've decided that printed menus are out; ditto for having my wait staff write orders on a notepad or commit them to memory. That's all too low tech. In fact, I don't even want my servers to submit orders using anything as basic as a been-there-done-that iPad, iPad mini, or any other type of handheld tablet. No, I want something *different*, something diners won't find anywhere else.

Knowing Synaptics' reputation for innovation, I meet with members of the company's UX (user experience) team, outline my vision, and ask what they can do for me. We toss a few ideas around, and eventually someone—it could be someone from their team, it could be me—comes up with the idea of turning the table itself into an ordering surface and more. Interesting idea . . . I decide I want to see what this might look like, and Synaptics goes off to its lab to figure out how to incorporate the features I want into the interface and create a prototype. In essence, I'm simply ordering a specific technology: I want a glass touchtop that offers a hundred different menu selections, and I want that menu to appear and then disappear, to be replaced by my choice of games, puzzles, videos, or scenic backdrops. And eventually, of course, the bill, complete with mobile payment options. Once the prototype is done, I sit down with the Synaptics team again, and we review it together, tweaking the design as needed—maybe we move the drinks selection to a different, swipeable "page" during one iteration and add a tic-tac-toe option to games in another. Or we play with the tabletop's color palette to ensure that the hues complement the surrounding decor. We do this again and again until we get it right. And in the end, I walk away with a touchscreen tabletop that looks cool, is intuitive, and brings my cutting-edge vision to life.

Human interface in action. And very much in keeping with the positioning statement we wrote for the company: *Synaptics is the leader in human interface solutions. With its innovative thinking, best-in-class technologies, and portfolio of integrated solutions, Synaptics empowers its partners to deliver intuitive user experiences.* Although such solutions already existed in the market and in fact Synaptics had innovated many of them, human interface was not considered a category per se since it is an embedded technology in other products from categories such as mobile phones, laptop computers, and sensors. So, we thought, why not just come out and claim leadership of this category right there in the positioning statement? It seems obvious now, but at the time, it was a simple aha! that emerged from the positioning exercise.

As with our previous case studies, the elevator story we created for Synaptics expands on the positioning statement:

> We are the pioneers and leaders of the human interface revolution, bringing innovative and intuitive user experiences to intelligent devices. From usability and R&D to supply chain and support, we collaborate with our partners to invent, build, and deliver human interface solutions that integrate seamlessly and elevate system value. The improved ease-of-use, functionality, and aesthetics of Synaptics-enabled products help make our digital lives more productive, secure, and enjoyable.

The Outcome

Synaptics's new brand and communication platform launched at the end of 2014. Alignment with the innovation message—inherent in the company's core values for all of its 30 years—remains the key to its success, and the messaging took a strong stance by positioning Synaptics as leading the human interface revolution as inventors, builders, and deliverers of innovative and intuitive user experiences. "The work that we did in terms of clarifying our corporate DNA was a critical foundation for the messages that we ultimately developed," said Ann Minooka, the head of global marketing communications and investor relations for Synaptics. "Following the positioning exercise, we developed a thought leadership platform that homed in on exactly what human interface is—what our vision is and what we mean when we use that phrase." Synaptics has used that platform as the basis for a variety of keynote addresses and for a presentation it gave at the Global Mobile Internet Conference, which is held annually in Beijing. "Positioning really helped us zero in on the messaging that we want to consistently convey," Minooka said. "And as a result, our visionary thought leadership story has been very well received."

Being seen as the human interface leader is imperative to Synaptics' long-term growth, and that is why the company works hard to maintain the trust and sense of partnership it has built up with clients over the years. "We don't have 200 customers or anything like that," said Bergman. "We have roughly 20 customers that matter, so we work really, really closely with them and try never to disappoint. And the outcome of that is the people who use our products tend to look to us first and say, 'All right, we're thinking about doing a flexible phone. What technologies do you have?' It's all about figuring out how we're going to interact with the future computing engines of the world."

It's also about figuring out how to use positioning as a guidepost for maintaining Mechanic culture internally as well as out in the market. And since innovation is woven throughout everything Synaptics does, it's no surprise to find that innovation is manifest throughout all aspects of the company's culture, particularly now that it has an even deeper understanding of its Mechanic soul. That soul shines through in internal hackathons organized to foster invention (winners are acknowledged at all-hands meetings and other events), on a celebrated patent wall, and in a demo room arrayed with finished products. It is evident in Bergman's in-house e-mails and online posts, including the thirtieth-anniversary blog, which notes the company's longstanding "dyed-in-the-wool commitment to enhancing how people interact with technology." And it shows up in the choices Synaptics makes in the companies it considers for merger and acquisition. That is why the company's purchase of Renesas SP Drivers (RSP), a unit of the Japanese chipmaker Renesas Electronics Corporation, makes perfect sense. The acquisition was a marriage of complementary Mechanics—both known for their engineering expertise—and allows Synaptics to integrate its touch technology with what Bergman calls RSP's "world-class" display drivers for smartphones and tablets.

Acquiring a fellow Mechanic, particularly one that allows it to expand its features offerings, makes communicating the company's mission and vision to new employees that much easier, especially when you understand how much your DNA type is a reflection of who you are as a company and how you get your message across. "When you grow a little bit each year by osmosis, people automatically learn the culture," said Bergman. "But when you inject 400 people in the midst of 70 percent of your employee population, as we did, suddenly you have to think about how you communicate, what you communicate, what their ideas are, and the fact that they have some preconceived notion of you even before they walk through the theoretical door."

Synaptics has had to go through quite a few transformations to get to where it is today, and Bergman foresees even more down the road as advances in technology continue to rewrite the human interface landscape. As for how he views that landscape, Bergman anticipates that virtual reality will be the next big frontier; he also sees great promise in the automotive and wearables fields as well as the Internet of Things. And although the semiconductor industry is no longer growing at the same historic rate as in the past, he notes that it's still a $350 billion business. "We're just shy of a $2 billion run rate now," he said. "We only have a 1 percent share, so there's a lot of opportunity out there for us to continue to grow." And with user experience playing an increasingly crucial role in next-generation applications, the company considers itself well positioned to remain the industry leader and, as Bergman wrote in the anniversary blog, "poised to drive the next inflection points of man and machine."

He notes that five years ago there wasn't one semiconductor company talking about human interface. "But that's what Synaptics is known for now," he said. "It's completely changed the way people perceive us in the industry."

13

Retrotope:
The Next Big Thing

DNA: Missionary

Genotype: Next Big Thing

The Challenge: When caught between a rock and a hard place, how to establish a scientific beachhead in the pharmaceutical industry with a new approach to fighting disease.

What could be better than being part of the Next Big Thing? Who wouldn't want to have a piece of a Next Big Thing company—an Apple, Amazon, Google, Netflix, or Salesforce—right on the cusp of its takeoff?

Making the leap from potential Next Big Thing to actual Next Big Thing can be a particularly fraught exercise, especially in the astronomically expensive, our-way-or-the-highway pharmaceutical arena. More often than not, researchers, scientists, and Big Pharma will have nothing to do with you or your big idea.

Retrotope Inc., a privately held clinical-stage pharmaceutical company based in Los Altos, California, faced that problem in its goal to change aging as we know it and put an end to the ravages of degenerative diseases such as Parkinson's and Alzheimer's. To achieve that objective, the company, which was incorporated in 2006, has been advancing a revolutionary unified theory of aging and degeneration that could result in dramatically new approaches to fighting disease. It also has created a new category of drugs composed of proprietary, reinforced compounds that both treat degenerative diseases and improve the quality of life as people age.

Retrotope's disease-modifying therapy consists of compounds that are chemically stabilized forms of essential nutrients. The company designed a new drug by making a tiny change to linoleic acid, a common and essential nutrient regularly ingested in food, after observing that a small alteration greatly fortified cells against lipid peroxidation, the damage that causes many diseases. Because the change is so small, the body functions normally and uses the reinforced linoleic acid as it normally would—except that the cells are "fireproofed" against the damage of degenerative diseases. In clinical tests the company has shown that when interacting with the altered linoleic acid, which is delivered in a fish-oil-like capsule, the cell membrane under assault from disease is modified to resist the damage. According to the company, the drug has limited or no side effects.

In short, Retrotope's therapies are capable of producing monumental change in the medical and pharmaceutical fields.

That was exactly the problem.

In addition to the fact that Retrotope's go-to-market story was long and complicated, with its most compelling aspects buried beneath often daunting scientific terms and data, an even bigger issue was that what the company offers is both new and unfamiliar. As a result, said Dr. Harry J. Saal, chairman of Retrotope's board of directors, it faced deep skepticism from pharmaceutical executives and investors who viewed Retrotope as too risky a venture.

Skepticism is a barrier Next Big Thing companies often face. We've talked about the naysaying that surrounded Steve Jobs' odds for success upon his 1997 return to Apple, but ridicule and scorn in the face of something new is, of course, nothing new. Henry Ford faced it down, as did one of his savvy investors, Horace Rackham, a Detroit lawyer who ignored the Michigan Savings Bank's advice to pass on purchasing Ford stock, since, it argued, "The horse is here to stay but the automobile is only a novelty—a fad." And while Thomas Edison turned a blind eye to the derision that greeted his countless failed efforts (said to number in the thousands) in pursuit of his most famous invention—only to have Henry Morton of the Stevens Institute of Technology dismiss his first commercial lightbulb with the prediction that it would be a "conspicuous failure"—he himself was guilty of the very same resistance when he disparaged Nikola Tesla's alternative power model, proclaiming that "Fooling around with alternating current is just a waste of time. Nobody will use it, ever." And then, of course, there's Digital Equipment Corp. founder Ken Olsen's 1977 famous misfire: "There is no reason for any individual to have a computer in his home."

Retrotope faced neither scorn nor ridicule; perhaps worse, no attention was paid to the new theory at all. In fact, getting a meeting with the right people at the right investment firms was proving to be a significant barrier. Without other companies doing—or at least talking about doing—something similar, it was as if Retrotope were operating in a vacuum. Like nature, most venture capitalists abhor a vacuum; few want to be first out of the gate when it comes to something new. "VCs don't want to invest in an industry where there aren't multiple companies to choose from," said Saal. "More than one choice allows them to say, 'Okay, great, there's a collective herd of companies attacking this problem. And it looks like maybe this one is better than that one, so here's where I'll invest my money.'" But when faced with just one industry option, they get cold feet. "There's a sense that it's just too weird and thus too risky."

To make matters worse, executives and investors also perceived the company's formula—which relies on a chemical workaround that uses broad-stroke methods to counteract degenerative conditions rather than eliminating specific problems at their source, the medical research community's preferred method for combating disease—as threatening to standard operating procedures, and perhaps even to careers. That put an interesting spin on the typical Next Big Thing hurdle. Whereas Missionaries such as Henry Ford, Steve Jobs, and Elon Musk probably heard (and ignored) comments such as "Don't waste your time, it can't be done," what Retrotope faced was more along the lines of "Don't waste your time, that's not how we do it."

What Retrotope found, according to Dr. Robert Molinari, cofounder and CEO of the company, was that even when potential investors were interested, they quickly got caught up in the issue of what the company was doing to address the perceived *cause* of a specific disease rather than what it was doing to avert the dysfunction. "Some people feel very strongly that you've got to start tackling a disease by focusing on the cause—that if you're not doing gene therapy, for example, then you're not curing the disease, or even fixing it," he said.

That meant that Retrotope's method was anything but popular. "Pick up any scientific magazine—*Nature*, say, or something from Stanford or any other research university—and you'll see that the trend in modern medicine is so-called precision medicine," said Dr. Charles Cantor, a Retrotope cofounder and National Academy of Sciences member. "That's where you study to death a particular disease and a particular pathway and carefully engineer something that attacks that one particular pathway. Which is great. The problem, however, is that we were coming in with something that was the opposite of that. And when we talked to drug companies and told people what we were doing, right away you'd see their brows furrow as if to say, 'No, no—that's not what we do. That's not the way we do science.'"

Retrotope, of course, was taking a different tack. Instead of working to eliminate specific diseases altogether, it was focusing its efforts on shutting down the ability of free radicals to do the damage that results in disease (not to mention aging). All diseases are a series of multiple steps, Saal explained; the question is, "Where along those steps do you intervene?" A proponent of precision medicine would say that you should step in at the beginning—you must repair the genetic defect or otherwise prevent a disease from occurring in the first place. But if you think of disease as a chain, he said, you realize that if you break any one of the links, you can break the chain. "It doesn't matter whether you break the first link, the last link, or the middle link. If you can break a link, you stop the process."

As an example, Molinari points to Friedreich's ataxia, a rare neurodegenerative disease for which Retrotope's drug RT001 has initiated clinical trials (there are currently no approved treatments for the condition). Without intervention, most patients can expect progressive loss of coordination and muscle strength, leading to motor incapacitation, the full-time use of a wheelchair, and ultimately an early death from cardiac complications. "If we can get patients walking, it means the disease has been modified," Saal said. "Yes, they'll still have the genetic defect, but it won't have a negative impact."

An additional benefit of the drug, at least in theory, lies in the fact that it is not Friedreich's ataxia–specific. Unlike precision drugs, where you take a certain drug for a certain condition and it targets it perfectly, Retrotope offers a horizontal drug, so to speak, meaning that—again, in theory—it could be used across a broad spectrum of diseases. I say "in theory" because Retrotope, which registered its drug as a pharmaceutical rather than a dietary supplement, is bound by law to administer the drug for specified uses only, and thus is unable to suggest it for off-label use once it is approved by the U.S. Food and Drug Administration (FDA). If Retrotope had registered the drug as a supplement, a regulatory gray zone, it would not have been subject to those governmental approval processes or rules, with consumers able to self-prescribe. But the downside to registering the formula as a supplement was the lack of serious attention that is given to the supplements industry. In many circles, supplements are seen as little more than elixirs, no better than snake oil.

To illustrate the effects of a so-called horizontal drug, Saal offers anti-inflammatories as an analogy: "You take aspirin or ibuprofen for many different things, because no matter the specific disease and no matter what part of the body it affects, many diseases share inflammation as a symptom. If you have inflammation, you take a pill, and the pill you take affects your whole body. You don't take this pill if the problem is in your stomach, that pill if it's in your arm, and that one over there if it's in your ankle. You dose the whole body, and hopefully the inflammation subsides, even if it doesn't necessarily fix the disease."

Retrotope's drug therapy works the same way in that it doesn't matter where in the body free-radical-caused degradation strikes: "We're not going to have a different version for heart problems and a different version for leg problems." And that, Saal said, is both uncomfortable and challenging for pharmaceutical companies. "They say, 'Why are you treating the whole body when the problem is in the heart?' The world is focused on certain approaches, and we're not doing it their way."

As if that weren't enough, Saal points out yet another layer of resistance that Next Big Thing companies such as Retrotope must overcome. "Imagine you're a foundation that has been giving grants for research of disease X, and for the last 10 years you've been giving grants in order to tackle the problem a certain way. Then someone comes along with a different approach. One reaction is to say, 'Wow, a breath of fresh air, let's try it!' But another, more common reaction is to respond, 'No, absolutely not, that's not the way we do things, and if I go along it's going to blow back on me.' They're invested in a certain worldview. Anything that challenges that worldview is not just a bad idea, it's threatening, it threatens their careers. Acknowledging that we have a viable approach is seen as denying the credibility of what they've been doing all along."

As a result, when Retrotope was looking for partners among large drug firms, its proposals tended to hit a wall. "Our business development people would meet with their business development people, and we'd hear, 'Oh, it sounds really interesting. Send us the presentation deck, and we'll circulate it inside the company.'" But that, said Saal, was nearly always the kiss of death for the proposal. Why? Because that "really interesting" deck was at some point sent for review to scientists wearing precision-medicine blinders that left them unable to absorb, much less envision, the Next Big Thing.

Retrotope also needed to overcome the perception that the company's outside-the-box solution was too good to be true, a perception, according to Saal, that had tainted the company with the dreaded "whiff of snake oil." The source of that whiff? A couple of things, starting with Retrotope's unconventional story. Typically, when pharmaceutical companies conduct research, they do it in their own laboratories or pay outside labs to do it for them. Either way, the companies own the results. As a small, angel-supported company that was short on funds, Retrotope had a research strategy that called for something different. Rather than pay to do its own research, the company manufactured limited amounts of the chemical compounds it wanted to study, and Dr. Mikhail Shchepinov, Retrotope's cofounder and chief science officer, whom Saal calls the "idea guy," delivered small quantities of the compound to researchers at various universities and labs around the world. (Saal also calls Shchepinov a modern-day Johnny Appleseed.) Recipients were free to use the chemical for experiments in whatever study areas they chose—Parkinson's, Alzheimer's, Friedreich's ataxia, diabetic retinopathies, and so on—making each research project a collaborative effort. In addition,

Retrotope gained significant financial leverage by supplying only a token amount of money for the experiments, with the rest coming from grants the individual researchers had received from the National Institutes of Health, the National Science Foundation, the Parkinson's Institute, and other organizations.

A side effect of this method, however, was that the resulting research was "all over the map," said Saal. "While high quality, the research wasn't designed the way a pharmaceutical company would investigate a compound; it wasn't investigated in great depth." Instead of initiating, say, 10 experiments, all focused on 1 disease, Retrotope ended up with the equivalent of 1 experiment for 10 different diseases. "When we collected all our research and presented to VCs, the reaction was, 'Wait a minute, this one compound is going to work with this and this and this?'" The answer was a resounding yes, but such results meant that Retrotope couldn't actually prove anything unless researchers combined data from different diseases, a process completely foreign to traditional pharmaceutical development. That made telling its story problematic (an issue common to the world of Missionaries, where an unconventional narrative can be par for the course).

Further complicating matters was the fact that the research also boasted data that seemed too good to be true. When Saal, who has a background in the physical sciences, first saw the data, he couldn't believe it. "I'm used to experimental data," he said, "and when you see an effect of, say, 30 percent, your reaction is, 'Wow! Thirty percent—that's great!' Because 30 percent *is* great." But Retrotope was seeing results of 100 percent efficacy, which was more than great; it was remarkable. As it turns out, it was too remarkable, if there is such a thing, "because it appeared almost as if someone were faking the data. The numbers were just off the charts."

An enviable problem—one any company would be happy to have—but a problem nonetheless. Retrotope knew that in addition to finding a way to reframe the issue of an outside-the-box drug bucking the scientific norm, it needed to rid itself of that snake oil whiff.

The Aha!

Unlike some of the companies featured earlier in this book, particularly our two (initially) reluctant Mothers (Tile and BuildingConnected), pinpointing Retrotope's DNA was never a problem. It was immediately apparent to everyone involved that the company was a Next Big Thing Missionary, one that had developed a drug platform that—thanks to its ability to preserve and restore mitochondrial and cellular health in degenerative diseases—could change and enhance the lives of millions. The issue instead was how to get that message out and, at the same time, overcome baked-in resistance to the company's raison d'être: essentially, how to recast the company's narrative about its disease-modifying therapy so that it would be more appealing to investors, clinical trial participants, and the press.

To that end, we first created a visionary positioning statement focused on the theory, not the drug—*Retrotope is leading the advance of a revolutionary new unified theory of aging and degeneration that can result in dramatically new approaches to therapy*—and then the following narrative, which now appears in some form on the company's home page:

> Pharmaceutical startup Retrotope is changing aging as we know it so that people do not have to suffer the ravages of many degenerative diseases. The company is leading the advance of a revolutionary new unified theory of aging and degeneration that can result in dramatically new approaches to therapy—a theory based on three groundbreaking discoveries:
>
> 1. Many degenerative diseases that were originally thought to be disparate actually share a common weakness.
>
> 2. That weakness is one type of chemical bond that makes membrane fats susceptible to oxidation damage and loss of function.

3. By strengthening that bond, we are able to prevent cellular damage.

Retrotope's category of new drugs are composed of proprietary, fortified nutrients that treat degenerative diseases and improve life as we age. Human trials of the company's first drug have shown promise in treating Friedreich's ataxia—a rare, neurodegenerative, and fatal genetic disease—and preclinical data support use of the drug category in major diseases such as Alzheimer's, Parkinson's, and diabetic retinopathies.

Untangling accessible data and messages from reams of statistics and jargon, though crucial, was just the first step. We determined that Retrotope also needed a story that encompassed a wide community of experts who would lend credibility to the company's groundbreaking theories and solutions and shift attention from the company as a lone voice shouting into the wind. Remember, as we noted in Chapter 4, there can be no category of one, no matter how revolutionary the Next Big Thing.

To that end, it needed experts who, despite the unconventional nature of the company's drug therapy, would support the notion that lipid peroxidation is indeed at the heart of many different diseases. The existence of this commonality across a wide range of diseases was not something that Retrotope should take credit for, appear to own, or defend alone. Instead, it needed to promote the message that there are other smart, credible people who view medical problems through a different lens and who understand that there may be alternative ways to solve them. "We understood that Retrotope can't be the only one saying these things," Saal said. "It all goes back to diversity of perspective. If you just try to solve problems one way—which is what the medical board is all about—you lose out on diversity of perspective."

Recent Alzheimer's research presents an example of that diversity of perspective, he said, pointing to studies highlighting the promise of therapeutic regimens that isolate neuroprotective agents to protect nerve cells from amyloid toxicity, which is believed to be a key player in the neurodegenerative mechanisms that underlie many diseases. "Everyone has been focused on a buildup in the brain of a particular artifact of Alzheimer's called beta amyloid," said Saal. "Countless billions of dollars have been spent trying to solve the beta amyloid problem, but they've had no success. And now researchers are discovering that you can have beta amyloids in the brain as long as you protect the neurons."

The Outcome

Retrotope has been using the new narrative on its website and with investors and the press. It also organized a successful roundtable with 30 scientists representing a variety of disciplines from both universities and pharmaceutical companies to discuss ideas about a new unified theory of aging. The goal was to create momentum behind a new way to look at medical problems so that it wouldn't feel foreign when outside-the-box companies such as Retrotope set out to secure funding or partner with foundations, research labs, universities, and other companies.

That is exactly what Retrotope aims to do. In November 2015, the company reconfirmed its alliance with the Friedreich's Ataxia Research Alliance and announced a partnership with the University of Florida for the opening of a clinical trial site to evaluate the safety, tolerability, pharmacokinetics, disease state, and exploratory endpoints of orally dosed RT001 in patients with Friedreich's ataxia.

Retrotope's strategy to penetrate the pharmaceutical industry takes advantage of the company's broader approach to the medical world while enabling it to maintain a focus on an orphan disease within it. Retrotope points to Friedreich's ataxia as a specific case in which it hopes its technology will reduce symptoms associated with the disease and in so doing suggests the potential it may have for treating other neurological conditions. By providing a living example of conducting science in both old and new ways, Retrotope is inching its way toward the Holy Grail of having its drug accepted as a horizontal drug that, like aspirin, can be used to treat a variety of conditions—in this case, many of the symptoms of disease and aging.

"We don't want this to just be a Retrotope story," Saal said. "It needs to be a movement to look at science in a new way. Getting people together in one room makes all the difference when you're trying to create a movement. The idea was to bring credible points of view together in a seminar setting to show that there's momentum behind this idea of looking at medical problems in a different way. We wanted to form a group that would not only take the ball and run with it outside of ourselves but also show that these researchers share a common vision—that they are invested in this other way of looking at the world."

He realizes it won't happen overnight, but what Saal envisions for the future is a brave new world of medicine in which patients can rely on a combination of therapies to treat disease, with researchers, investors, and others no longer wedded to the idea that there is only one way to do things. In short, a world in which Retrotope is no longer the Next Big Thing.

14

OpenGov:
Charisma in Action

DNA: Missionary

Genotype: Cult of Personality

The Challenge: In a market that doesn't always embrace new technologies, how to bring a vision of better technology to government.

I knew that Zachary Bookman, the CEO of OpenGov—the leader in government performance management technology—was a Cult of Personality Missionary almost immediately. But it wasn't until an appointment at the company's Redwood City, California, headquarters that that conclusion hit home for one of my colleagues. Our meeting with Michael Schanker, head of marketing, was already under way—with Zac scheduled to join us as soon as he was free—when Schanker glanced through an open door of the conference room and announced, "Yep, Zac is in the building."

There wasn't one person in the room who hadn't met Zac at least a couple of times before, but that didn't stop any of us from turning from what we were doing to peer through the open doors of the conference room. Those of us with our backs to the doors swiveled in our chairs to find him. He blew into the room a few minutes later with a flurry of greetings and apologies for having been delayed by a meeting that ran late. With his arrival, the energy in the room shifted in an instant from post-lunch relaxed to full-on "Zac Attack."

And there, in a nutshell: a Cult of Personality Missionary.

In typical Cult of Personality fashion, however, Zac's path to becoming a Missionary was anything but linear—or typical. Before colaunching OpenGov in 2012, he served as an anticorruption advisor to U.S. Army Lieutenant General H. R. McMaster. The general, who would go on to serve as National Security Advisor in the Trump administration, headed the government transparency task force at the headquarters of the International Security Assistance Force, a NATO-led security mission, in Kabul, Afghanistan. Zac was brought on to advise on the rule of law and governance. A graduate of Yale Law School, he had practiced trial litigation at a prestigious San Francisco law firm and before that had served as a law clerk on the U.S. Court of Appeals for the Ninth Circuit. Zac earned a master's degree in public administration from the Harvard Kennedy School and studied corruption in Mexico as a Fulbright Fellow after the passage of that country's Freedom of Information Act.

His zeal for government and the way it functions—he once taught an American government course at San Quentin State Prison—stretches back to his childhood. Zac's father, who is passionate about improving a community's quality of life, advised federal and congressional agencies in his work for the National Academy of Sciences in Washington, D.C.; he later took a job with the Seattle Department of Transportation when Zac was in college. All of that gave his son a front-row seat to the workings of bureaucracy, both good and bad, from an early age.

Although Zac's background may not have much in common with that of the average tech-steeped CEO, he embodies the mission-driven entrepreneurial spirit ingrained within many of them, particularly those who are Cult of Personality leaders. Although plenty of kids earn money from babysitting, dog walking, and paper routes, Zac and his brother, Tyras, who is three years older, took entrepreneurship to a different level. "I started mowing lawns with Ty when I was eight and then took over the business when he went to college," he said. All told, Zac had saved about $50,000 by the time he left for school. His next venture was a small investment fund made up of "friends, family, and fools" while he was an undergraduate at the University of Maryland, College Park. Like so many others, the fund lost money during the dot-com crash of 2001, teaching its manager a few lessons along the way.

Many more lessons came during Zac's anticorruption studies in Mexico and, later, when he was putting those and other lessons to use during his eight months in Afghanistan—including the importance of being clear-eyed about what works and what doesn't in government, especially local government. As he noted in an op-ed piece he wrote for the *New York Times* in 2012 after a tour of the Shah Wali Kot District in the northern area of Kandahar Province, despite the fact that "rule of law efforts focus on the provision of formal justice" at NATO headquarters and neighboring installations, in the end "international rule of law efforts seem disconnected from the needs and realities of rural Afghanistan."

Zac wears his curly black hair long, nearly down to his shoulders. Coupled with a closely groomed beard, it is a look that allowed him to blend in whenever he ventured out from the relative safety of the 25-foot walls of the military base that housed the task force. Ever on the lookout for Taliban kidnappers during his occasional excursions around Kabul or when traveling in the countryside, he never let his hand stray too far from his concealed Beretta 9 mm pistol, one of the weapons he'd been required to learn to use at the Blackwater training site in South Carolina—the private military company is now called Academi—before his arrival.

Far less on edge these days, Zac exudes the cheerful, easygoing vibe of a surfer. He took up the sport one summer during graduate school, when he and a friend drove from Los Angeles to Costa Rica in an old Jeep Cherokee, camping and surfing their way down the Pacific Coast. That adventurous spirit also saw him hitchhike from England to Africa while he was a visiting student at Oxford and led him to climb Mount Kilimanjaro in Tanzania (16,000 feet), Margherita Peak in Uganda (16,762 feet), and Denali in Alaska (20,310 feet). A four-time Washington, D.C., champion wrestler in high school, he has run the Marine Corps marathon and recently completed his first 50-mile ultramarathon. Even at work, engaged in an adventure of a different sort, it's clear from the way he's constantly moving—even jumping up to take over a keyboard during a meeting when his ideas spilled out faster than the laptop's owner could type—that Zac isn't happy when he's stuck behind a desk for too long; that is why he's been known to skateboard around the company parking lot while conducting business on the phone.

While still in Afghanistan, where Zac worked out of a sparsely furnished tin shed by day and occupied a bunk bed in a moldy shipping container he shared with two American soldiers at night, he was collaborating with future OpenGov colleagues and advisors, including cofounder Joe Lonsdale, who is now the company chairman. (Lonsdale is also a cofounder of Addepar, another data-mining company and the Value Mechanic case study featured in Chapter 11.) One thing led to another, and the group ended up in conversations with the government administrators of a prominent Silicon Valley city, ultimately offering to analyze the California city's budget data for years-long patterns and trends, information that they could then share with others online.

The officials were enthusiastic, but the project hit a wall when it became apparent that no one on the government end knew how to produce clean budget data, which was buried within a decades-old enterprise resource planning (ERP) software system. In light of the time and expense it would take to retrieve the information manually—it turns out the municipality was $10 million into the ERP system, which was originally delivered on 20 disks—it might as well have been stored on the moon.

"We realized that the people running the city—smart, good-hearted people—couldn't access the data to see where money was going across very complicated enterprises," said Zac, who by this time had returned to California to build the company. Too much of the data was simply inaccessible. "Because of the way the system was set up, they couldn't share information with the elected officials who needed it to govern. Their own staff, tasked with fighting fire and crime and delivering water and power, didn't have the data to make good decisions."

And not just in that one city, obviously; the problem is endemic to governments of all sizes and levels. A large percentage of the data generated by the tens of thousands of governments across the nation (and that's not even taking into account the rest of the world) is buried within archaic, difficult-to-access silos, rendering it virtually inaccessible. Staff can't see it, and neither can the public. As a result, said Zac, "Citizens are losing trust and becoming disengaged."

Although there are many problems in government that involve politics, red tape, and institutional incentives, the team realized that what they were facing was nothing more than a technology problem, albeit a really big one. "We thought, 'We can solve this problem,'" said Zac. Even more, they realized, "We have to solve it."

The mission-driven statement "We have to solve it" is classic Missionary. Whereas a Mother wants to solve the problem on behalf of her overwhelmed customers and a Mechanic focuses on its technical ability to provide the products needed to solve it, only a Missionary would have a driving mission to bring better data analysis to government to serve the greater good.

Thus was born the vision of a suite of solutions that maps to the life cycle of government management, including how governments plan, operate, and communicate internally and with elected bodies and citizens. The OpenGov platform opens a window onto countless details about government spending and performance—everything from how much city council members were paid over a 10-year period in Chicago versus Boston to how much a local police department spends annually on its canine unit or to what it cost six years earlier to rebuild the kennel that houses those dogs. The system is built on top of the tens of thousands of on-premise legacy ERP accounting and other back-office systems that are used by every city, county, school district, special district, and state agency in the country, making it simple to extract data that were previously difficult to retrieve. Once the data have been pulled from those systems and are in the cloud, the company offers applications that assist in building budgets and management reporting and renders the data searchable, sortable, and analyzable down to the last penny—all in service to greater government efficiency, effectiveness, and transparency. Simply put, everything is made easier because all the data are organized in a user-friendly manner and are accessible in real time.

"Our mission is to enable our customers to be successful," said Schanker, the marketing head of OpenGov, which has raised $77 million over the last few years and is backed by Andreessen Horowitz (Marc Andreessen also sits on the board), Emerson Collective, 8VC, and Thrive Capital. "We're offering them a better way to do their jobs."

When most people consider government, he said, "they think about federal government, they think about bureaucracy, and they think about polarization. They think, 'You're never gonna get anything done.' But that's the furthest thing from what we're talking about and doing at OpenGov. When you get to the local level, it's really very simple. Do we want more public safety? Do we want safe streets? Do we want our potholes filled? Do we want good schools for our children? Do we want potable drinking water?"

"In most cases, the answer is yes," he said. "But how do you get there? And what are all the trade-offs that have to be made to get there? These are the kinds of things we are enabling people to figure out more effectively. When it comes to local government administration, there aren't always straightforward answers. You never have as many dollars as you have good ideas to improve the community. But local governments are the laboratories of democracy, so we're helping people make more informed and more data-driven decisions instead of acting on gut feel and a paper report that took three weeks to generate and is riddled with errors."

Schanker added, however, that the company is not out to change the face of government. "What we're doing is offering technology that makes it easier for these people to be their best selves. The administrative problems they face on a daily basis? They've already been solving those problems even without our technology. It's just that it's been a much more painful process—a slower, more manual process. The time they save using OpenGov lets them spend more time on strategy and problem solving, which in turn leads to better outcomes for the communities they serve."

As OpenGov increases its client base to thousands of governments—as of June 2017, its platform had been adopted by 1,500 administrations across 48 states, and the company is on the brink of international expansion—the goal is to network the platform to allow users to learn from one another and share ideas, problems, and solutions. It also enables administrators to compare themselves with similarly sized entities as they build budgets and establish performance benchmarks in management reporting. Not only does the network increase the adoption rate, the stickiness, and the value of OpenGov, it also is building the world's largest repository of public sector financial and performance data.

Nonetheless, when it comes to problem solving, OpenGov's customers are the ones doing the heavy lifting. "We're just providing them with the tools and utility to do it," Schanker said. "That's why we say we're *powering* more effective and accountable government, not that we're *creating* more effective and accountable government."

In the same way that OpenGov avoids any suggestion that it is out to do anything more than empower those dedicated to effecting better government, it is careful to steer clear of politics in this age of deep political polarization, particularly at the national level. Although many of the people who work for OpenGov are passionate about government and hold strong political views on both sides of the aisle, the company's mission is 100 percent apolitical. "Local government is not about politics," Schanker said. "It's about public administration. Democrat versus Republican just doesn't mean much at the local level."

Whatever their degree of political engagement, administrators at all levels of government are advocating for more effective and accountable government and have sought out the OpenGov platform. Others, however, are either unaware of its potential or are so deeply entrenched in the status quo that they are afraid of change. How, then, to bring a vision of better bureaucracy to an often static market that isn't always open to new technologies?

The Aha!

Zac already was acting as a Cult of Personality leader within the company, even if before the positioning exercise no one was able to put a label on exactly what it was he brought to the table. Although he was doing it subconsciously, he already was using his Cult of Personality as a tool to inspire and drive his employees, who were attracted to him and his company and shared his passion for enabling better government. "Everyone here understands there's a significant element of this company that is mission-driven," said Schanker. "And most people, including me, choose to work at OpenGov because they believe in the mission."

Before he started at OpenGov in late 2016, Schanker wasn't looking to leave his previous job; in fact, he was happy and doing well. Nonetheless, when a headhunter approached him about the position, the more he heard about OpenGov, the more he found himself drawn to learning more about a company driven by a mission of transforming the way government works and in doing so having an impact on something bigger than itself. Meeting Zac clinched the deal. "It was clear he was describing something that was much more than a product," Schanker said. "It was also clear that he was the standard-bearer for the mission and message and that there was a huge opportunity to get him out there delivering it. As a marketer, that was a big part of why I took the role."

The trick now was to find a way to use that Cult of Personality tool externally to build the company and beyond that to build a movement for change (i.e., more open, effective, and accountable government) on a massive scale. Starting, of course, with selling the executive team—particularly the CEO—on the idea of using Zac's Cult of Personality as a positioning tool, a means of launching the message of better government through the OpenGov platform.

It actually turned out to be fairly easy. Although a casual discussion with the C-suite before the positioning exercise revealed that OpenGov considered itself predominantly customer-focused—despite the fact that it was marketing itself as a Value Mechanic by highlighting the company's ability to provide a superior product in the form of a platform that simplified data access—the DNA and genotype tests quickly showed the management team that the company was actually a Missionary whose primary goal was to deliver revolutionary change in the form of better government. (Not surprisingly, the Jungian brand archetype that came up most often for the management team was the Magician.)

Persuading Zac to embrace and align with the Cult of Personality designation took a little more time because of the baggage that can surround the term. In fact, when I approached him about using

OpenGov as a case study, his main concerns were that he not be painted as a "narcissist and a sociopath"—he most certainly is neither of those—and that the team's accomplishments not be undervalued or overshadowed. He came to see, however, that acting as their best selves, Cult of Personality Missionary leaders lead by making heroes out of customers and serving as champions for their organizations. He came to understand the value of initiating a better-government movement with him at the center—of using his Cult of Personality to realize a vision of government that runs more smoothly, more transparently, more openly, and with every bit of data exactly where you need it when you need it.

All of which we encapsulated in the positioning statement and elevator story we created for the company:

- **Position:** *OpenGov is the leader in government performance management technology: easy-to-use cloud software for better budgeting, improved reporting and operational intelligence, and comprehensive transparency and open data.*

- **Elevator Story:** *OpenGov is the leader in government performance management technology: easy-to-use cloud software for better budgeting, improved reporting and operational intelligence, and comprehensive transparency and open data. OpenGov solutions give governments the right tools and relevant data for more informed decision making and better outcomes for the public.*

The Outcome

OpenGov's next step in bringing that vision into the full light of day grew out of our understanding that the company should promote its Zac-led movement by taking a cue from Salesforce and building an ecosystem around its platform the way Marc Benioff has done with his company's annual Dreamforce. An OpenGov conference, which is in the early planning stages, will be like going to TED: it will bring together customers from governments around the world, developers, and consultants; feature keynote speakers (including Zac, who will have a chance to illustrate his vision of better and more open, effective, and accountable government), government officials, and community representatives; and give users an opportunity to attend panel discussions and breakout sessions, learn about new products, attend training sessions, and earn certifications.

Even more, it will enable a physical gathering of the OpenGov network, the online community the company is currently building, which will enable users to discuss problems, suggest solutions (online or over the phone), and call on technology that will allow them to compare their cities, states, regions, or countries with others of similar size. Although the beauty of OpenGov's developing network lies in the fact that government administrators throughout the country and around the world can share best practices online without having to communicate in person or even in real time, nothing can replace the power of face-to-face interactions when it comes to finding creative solutions to the thorniest problems.

Zac can leverage his Cult of Personality to bring those in charge of government planning and budgeting to OpenGov's version of the Promised Land. And we got him to believe it, too, all in service to his vision. Although initially dubious, Zac has settled into and even embraced the idea of acting as a Cult of Personality Missionary leader of a movement.

Referring to the methodology we used to get him there, he noted that the positioning exercise offered far more than branding alone ever could have done. "This was not marketing communications positioning as a thought exercise," he said. "It was how do we build a company? How do we disrupt an industry? And how do we create market leadership and dominance? We now know that we want to create a message that can go viral. We know that we want to establish a category that can differentiate us from the competition. And we know that we want to create a guiding light—a North Star—that will rally the entire company around a shared set of messages and positions and principles that will allow us to work in lockstep and move at a more rapid and effective pace."

And there's nothing like a Cult of Personality Missionary leader to make it happen.

Conclusion

Defining your company clearly and succinctly and understanding why it matters in the market is no longer a mystery. Now you know that you can discover your positioning DNA and use it to answer the toughest questions in business: "Who are you?" and "Why do you matter?" Once you know at your core if your company is a Mother, a Mechanic, or a Missionary, you'll have the power to get to aha! and develop a perfect positioning statement that differentiates you from the competition and compels customers to come calling. You'll be able to leverage those innate characteristics to achieve alignment and get all your canoes paddling in the same direction.

Why? Because companies are like people. They have DNA that is reflected in their behaviors. Just as knowing who you are at your core enables you to be a better you, leaders who understand their positioning DNA can use it to their advantage and be better at marketing and selling their products.

Marketing is, after all, a Holy Grail effort to influence opinion and change behavior so that companies can sell more stuff. But none of that can happen if you haven't nailed the positioning. Once you do and get to aha!, you'll have the epicenter of great marketing under your thumb.

All you have to do at that point is build a thoughtful message architecture that appeals to both the rational and the emotional sides of your customers and create a compelling corporate narrative around that positioning to tell your story. Then you treat that story like a virus and inject it into every single communication channel to which you have access so that you can infect the market with your unique position. Build your digital footprint and be relentless in the consistency and frequency of your message. Before long, you'll see that you've gone from message architecture to market resonance—and it all started with a DNA-based positioning statement. This is how the tiny get mighty and the mighty get powerful. So get going! Get to aha!

Acknowledgments

This book took me 30 years to accomplish. I always wanted to write it, but work and life took precedence. Then I met Joe DiNucci, an accomplished business coach and partner in Enabling Thought Leadership, a small consultancy designed to help authors get their books done. He did exactly that. Thank you, Joe. And thank you, Lauren Cuthbert, who captured my voice and was at my side throughout the project, ghostwriting and editing. Thanks also to Ron Ricci, John Volkmann, and Jeremy Hartman, who worked for me at Cunningham Communication in the 1980s and 1990s and provided some of the idea nuggets here that grew and blossomed in the intervening years. And thanks to the gang, both past and present, at Cunningham Collective, who improve the process every day. Specifically, thanks to Becky Bausman, who pulled together my theories into a coherent framework; to Leon Hunt, who recognized the importance of the project to me and to the company, and paved the way; to Victoria Graham, who added so much to the branding framework; to Lee Bellon, who helped with the artwork; and to Henry

Hwong, who stepped up his leadership so I could do this. Thanks also to my mentor, Regis McKenna, who is a positioning genius. And to Al Ries and Jack Trout, who invented the practice in 1969 and made it credible. Thanks to my many clients over the years for whom I practiced positioning and got better at my craft on their dime. And to Steve Jobs, who stretched me beyond my limits and allowed me to help him change the world. Special thanks also to the clients who allowed me to tell their stories in these pages: Dustin DeVan and Zac Hays, Mike Farley, Eric Poirier, Rick Bergman and Ann Minooka, Harry Saal, Zac Bookman and Mike Schanker. And to all of my friends and former clients who put their stamp on this treatise: Christopher Michel, Guy Kawasaki, Walter Isaacson, Steve Blank, Reed Hastings, Geoffrey Moore, Bill Davidow, David Kelley, Esther Dyson, Andy Kessler, Stewart Alsop, Rich Moran, Katie Hafner, Steve Swasey, Kelly Close and Marty Beard. And, of course, to The Amazing Richard. And finally to my husband, Rand Siegfried, and my children, McKinley and Cormac Siegfried. You guys have always been there for me. I love you this much!

Index

About the Author

 An entrepreneur at the forefront of marketing, branding, positioning, and communicating the Next Big Thing, Andy Cunningham has played a key role in the launch of a number of new categories, including video games, personal computers, desktop publishing, digital imaging, RISC microprocessors, software as a service, very light jets, and clean tech investing. She is an expert in creating and executing marketing, branding, and communication strategies that accelerate growth, increase shareholder value, and advance corporate reputation.

Andy came to Silicon Valley in 1983 to work for Regis McKenna and help Steve Jobs launch the original Macintosh. When Steve left Apple to form NeXT and acquire Pixar, he chose Andy's public relations agency, Cunningham Communication, to represent him. She continued to work with Steve for several years and has developed marketing, branding, and communication strategies for game-changing technologies and companies ever since.

Andy is the founder and president of Cunningham Collective, a marketing, brand strategy, and communication firm dedicated to bringing innovation to market. The firm has worked with many companies in various markets, including telecommunications, search, energy efficiency, media and publishing, finance, mobile apps, display technology, healthcare, big data, and semiconductors. Andy is also the host of the popular podcast Marketing Over Ice (www.moi.fm).

Andy graduated from Northwestern University and lives on a 1932 wooden boat in Sausalito, California, with her husband Rand Siegfried.

Web: www.cunninghamcollective.com/ and www.get2aha.com
LinkedIn: www.linkedin.com/in/andreacunningham